FOREVER
in Our Hearts

MAUREEN O'NEILL HOOKER

Copyright © 2023 Maureen O'Neill Hooker.

All rights reserved.

No part of this book may be used or reproduced in any manner whatsoever without written permission of the author, except in the case of brief quotations for review.

 Year of the Book
135 Glen Avenue
Glen Rock, PA 17327

ISBN: 978-1-64649-360-9 (paperback)
ISBN: 978-1-64649-361-6 (ebook)

Library of Congress Control Number: 2023915088

All scripture is taken from the Holy Bible, New International Version®, NIV® Copyright ©1973, 1978, 1984, 2011 by Biblica, Inc.® Used by permission. All rights reserved worldwide.

Contents

Prologue		1
1	The Dream	3
2	Reality	7
3	Grief Counseling	13
4	The Police Report	17
5	The Phone	23
6	Regrets	29
7	Remembering Joe	33
8	In the Beginning	39
9	Leaving the Nest	45
10	Texas Hold'em	53
11	The Elephant in the Room	59
12	The Move to Las Vegas	65
13	Fibromyalgia, the Mystery Disease	73
14	A Party to Remember	79
15	Stem Cell Transplant	83
16	The New Normal	91
17	Life in Remission	95
18	The Land of Maureen	103
19	Perception and Reality	109
20	Bargaining	113

21 | What We Didn't Know 119
22 | Trust in the Lord 125
23 | Ever-Present Grief 129
24 | Island Time 131
25 | Joe Is Still with Me 135

Prologue

December 28, 2018

"Please help me, God. I have prayed and asked others to pray. I have been to counseling both outside and inside the church. I have waited patiently for your divine guidance, but I still have no idea how to help my son, Joe. You were there when he was created, there when he was born, and you've been there for every moment of his life. You love him as much as I do, and he is as much your son as he is mine. I don't know what else to do, God. Everything I have tried has failed. Only you know what is right for him. I am giving him back to you."

I was lying in my bed, so worried about Joe that I was unable to sleep. I had no strength to continue on my own. God was my only hope, and I was praying with all I had left. I was looking for peace of mind.

I must have dozed off, because suddenly I found myself climbing a mountain with Joe beside me. The rocks, the sky, and even the air was the color of desert sand and stones. Suddenly, like Abraham of old with his son Isaac, I was bringing my son to God, trusting God with Joe's future.

Just a minute ago in my prayer, I had said I was letting go, that I was going to stop striving and trust Him to fix whatever was wrong. But I was always second-guessing myself. Could I really let go and let God this time?

Yes. I had done all I could. I was finished.

A strong gust of wind blew against me, and as I struggled to stay upright, I suddenly heard a child's voice say, "Even unto death?"

I stopped.

That couldn't have been God, I reasoned, because his voice would have shaken the earth like thunder. This was more like someone saying, "I can't believe you would give me to God. Even if it means my death?"

It could have been Joe, but I did not spend time on that thought because the death question had to be a trick. God is in charge of life and death, not me. Without God, I'm not even capable of taking a breath. Besides, when Abraham surrendered his son, God did not let the boy die. Angels came to save Isaac because Abraham trusted God. All I had to do was trust Him too.

In the nanosecond it took for those thoughts to flash through my mind, the little voice asked again, "Even unto death?"

"Yes!" I answered. "Even unto death, and I promise you, God, I will never second-guess what you decide to do with Joe."

The words of Proverbs 3:5 filled my mind: "Trust in the LORD with all your heart and lean not on your own understanding."

Then the impenetrable dust around me faded to black.

1 The Dream

Joe was fifty-one years old when I gave him back to God. The dream I had that night was so real it startled me awake with an internal explosion that jolted through me like a seizure. It felt as though a fierce thing were beating and punching me, trying to get out of my body. I was sure I was dying. Everything hurt—behind my eyes hurt, the root of every hair on my head hurt, my bones, my flesh, my fingernails hurt. Every cell of my body was on fire, separately and simultaneously. I was convinced I was dying.

I woke up twisting and moaning, trying to yell, trying to alert Jim, my husband, so he could call an ambulance. I knew that if I lived long enough to get to the hospital, I would need to describe the pain. It was worse than a ten. Still, the words in my heart were, "Trust in the Lord. Lean not on your own understanding."

Finally, fully awake, I sat up. I didn't think I could stand or walk, yet I had no trouble swinging my legs over the edge of the bed and getting up. I stood there for a moment, shocked that, despite what I had just experienced, I seemed to be okay. I woke Jim and told him we had to go to urgent care right away. Whatever had just happened, I couldn't live through another night like this one.

We spent the next several hours at the emergency room. When all was said and done, the doctor gave me a brace for my broken kneecap (from a fall on December 16, incidentally Joe's birthday) and a prescription for pain relief. It was afternoon by the time we filled the prescription and headed home.

Minutes later, the screen on my cell phone lit up, "Unknown caller."

Telemarketer, I thought. *I won't answer.*

But as I fumbled to silence the phone, a man's voice said, "Is this Maureen Hooker?"

"Yes."

"Are you the mother of Joseph Patrick Hooker in Las Vegas?"

"Yes."

"Where are you?"

"Greenville, North Carolina."

I put the phone on speaker, and Jim pulled to the side of the road. An officer from the Las Vegas Police Department identified himself by name and badge number and said, "Joseph called 911 at 10:55 this morning to report a shooting in his apartment." With a bit of quick math, I realized it was just after 11:00 A.M. in Las Vegas.

The officer had arrived at the apartment within minutes. Nothing seemed out of order, he told us, but the front door was ajar. Before attempting to enter, he went to the manager's office to check the lease application, where he found my name and phone number listed as the emergency contact. The officer then asked if there was anything he should be concerned about before entering Joe's apartment.

"What do you mean?" I asked. "What could you be worried about?"

"Death by cop," he answered. "It's a type of suicide where a person calls 911 to say there's an emergency with a gun involved. A SWAT team rushes to the scene and breaks down the door, only to face someone who is armed and waiting to be killed."

Jim and I looked at each other in horror. "No. He won't hurt you. Please, don't hurt him. Don't scare him," I begged. "He's sick. He has multiple myeloma, a type of blood cancer. It's a fatal disease. He would never hurt anyone."

"I will check on your son and call you back."

Jim tried to ask questions, but the officer said, "You have my name, badge ID number, and phone number. I have to go to my men. This is an active crime scene; someone will call you as soon as possible."

We immediately called Joe, but his voicemail answered. Jim called the officer back, but he didn't answer. We called Joe again and again, and when we were finally able to think, we drove home. Jim continued to call the police department every twenty minutes to ask the same question: "Please, tell us if our son is injured. You must know something!" They continued to say they couldn't give us any information. Every person Jim spoke to promised to call as soon as they had something to tell us.

At home, I turned on CNN and googled the local TV news in Las Vegas to see if there was any information. No luck. Minutes became hours. We were eventually told the officer who had originally contacted us had left that scene and was now at a different crime scene. They repeated that he would call us when he had time; they were polite but unyielding.

After four hours, the phone rang. It was an investigator assigned to the coroner's office, a wonderful, sensitive, and caring person named Brittani. She told us she had been with Joe in his apartment for two hours, and she was now driving back to the office with her report. She said Joe's phone, wallet, computer, and car keys were with him, but his car could not be found. She'd had no trouble identifying him from his driver's license. We talked for a long time.

Brittani advised us not to fly out to Las Vegas because there was nothing we could do. Everything would soon be closed for New Year's, and Joe could not be moved to a funeral home until after the medical examiner's autopsy, which would not happen until after the holiday.

She told us the police department used several approved funeral homes in rotation and told us where Joe would be taken after the autopsy. We would have one week after Joe's arrival at that mortuary to choose a different funeral home if we wanted. We asked about his belongings, but they couldn't be released until we presented a legal document establishing our right to have them.

It was the evening of December 29, 2018. Our son had died by his own hand, according to the police—and that was all we knew. All thoughts of the way I'd awakened that morning, of the hours spent at urgent care, and even of my prayer the night before were gone.

2 Reality

It wasn't until Joe died that we realized how little we knew about his life. He lived alone and did not leave a note. Only 20 percent of the people who end their lives leave an explanation. I imagine they're convinced that no one would understand how desperate they are.

We knew Joe had been working for a large furniture company that remodeled hotels, but we were unaware that the brand he represented had been discontinued and his contract had been cancelled. He'd only told us he was angry that he wouldn't be receiving the commission he'd been working on for more than a year, and his only option was to collect unemployment... which he hated.

We had agreed to supplement his income for six months, but he'd only asked for $400 a month. We knew that wouldn't even cover his car payment, never mind rent, phone, etc.—but we didn't send more than his request.

I had asked him to sign up for COBRA, the law that allows terminated employees to continue their workplace health insurance for the gap between jobs. I told him we'd pay for it, and he didn't argue. But I didn't nag, and when he didn't tell us how much it would cost, I knew he hadn't done anything. Administrative tasks were not his strong suit. I let it go.

I wanted him to find something with benefits ASAP. To me, a job with good benefits was the most important thing he could have. He must not have agreed, because he never mentioned benefits or salary or anything else about work. Once when he called for money,

I was in the middle of doing something, and I asked, "Is your need dire?"

He chuckled. "Isn't it always dire?"

A counselor had told me that I was overfunctioning (doing something for someone who needed to do things for himself), but I didn't know how to stop.

After Joe's death, as information dribbled in, we learned that *dire* was an understatement. Eventually, his license plate number appeared on a list of impounded cars that had been repossessed on December 20, 2018, nine days before he died. We had spoken with him two or three times after the twentieth, and he had not mentioned the car. In fact, I had purchased a Whole Foods cooked "Christmas Dinner for Four" that he told me he had taken to a friend's house on Christmas Eve.

On January 2, 2019, the coroner's office called to say that one of his friends had gone to his apartment to check on him and called the number on the yellow crime tape to ask how to reach Joe's family. The coroner gave us the number of Joe's former boss and close friend, David, who was instantly solicitous and sympathetic. During our conversation, we mentioned the word "suicide," and David dropped the phone.

He told us he had teased Joe about his food choices, saying, "You're killing yourself," and when he saw the yellow police tape, he'd presumed Joe had died of a heart attack. We learned that David's birthday was three days after Joe's, and during their eight years of friendship, they had often celebrated their birthdays and Christmas together.

When his car was repossessed, Joe told David's wife, Jenna, that it was in the shop, and asked her to give him a ride to Whole Foods to pick up his contribution to their Christmas Eve dinner. They sent us pictures of Joe's last birthday and Christmas.

David agreed to act as our representative and went into Joe's apartment for us. We watched as he and Jenna used the camera on his cell phone to show us what was in the drawers and the closets.

They packed up the pictures and things that we said were important and meaningful and sent them to us. They treated us like family, and we remain profoundly grateful.

It was hard to accept that Joe had taken his own life, and I spent a lot of time thinking that maybe he had been murdered instead. He'd been a professional gambler, so it seemed plausible to me that he might have died due to a gambling debt. Although there was nothing to support my opinion, I imagined that someone had forced him to make the 911 call and staged his death.

My blood turned to sludge; I often found myself blank, empty of thoughts, unsure of what I was looking at. My ears were full of white noise, and my senses felt disengaged from the earth. Still, God held me up, and I trusted him to help me understand . . . someday. Every time I was at my wit's end, those familiar words came back to me: "Trust in the Lord with all your heart and lean not on your own understanding."

On the day that Joe died, we had endless conversations with our two adult daughters, Tammy and Jennifer, and we talked to a lot of friends and relatives. That day ended and another began, but I don't remember much. I was numb. Over the next few days, snow and ice grounded air travel on the East Coast, and drivers were told to stay off the roads.

Jennifer brought her lifelong friends, Sandra and Nancy, home with her, and they stayed together in our guest bedroom as though they were having a slumber party from years long gone. We hung out and played Scrabble the way we used to . . . when Joe was there to beat us.

My brother, Barry, and his wife, Jane, drove through the blizzard all the way from Rhode Island. Barry put two books in my hand and said, "These helped me during a very hard time. I hope they can help you." I don't think I ever thanked him properly, but those books remain beside my bed, the pocket-sized *Enchiridion* by Epictetus, a Greek philosopher born a slave more than two thousand years ago, whose philosophy is similar to the "Serenity Prayer." The other book, *Courage under Fire*, was by Admiral James B. Stockdale, who credits Epictetus with helping him survive more than seven years as a POW in the Hanoi Hilton. After Joe's death, I couldn't read for a long time.

Our friends, Steve and Susan, left work and came straight to our home when they heard the news. I will never forget how we stood in a circle and hugged each other while we prayed.

On January 11, 2019, we held a memorial service at our church. We had pictures of Joe and beautiful music, and Jim and I gave communion to everyone there. Jim said a lot of wonderful things about our son, and Jennifer wrote an amazing eulogy; I will never know how she managed to read it. We had a reception at the church social hall and invited everyone back to our home for comfort food. It was a long, surreal day, but I lived.

Jim and I had preplanned our funerals a few years earlier, and we had selected a lovely spot where our ashes were to be buried. When Joe died, we met with our funeral director, to see if there was room for Joe there. There wasn't, so we purchased a place at the top of a new columbarium in the middle of a memorial garden. We decided to have a family ceremony there with a pastor the next time we were all together.

In the meantime, I had a long sofa table in front of the window in my kitchen where my orchids thrived. When we received Joe's ashes, they rested with the orchids, beside an angel with a poem engraved on it that Jim's sister had sent us: "If tears could build a stairway, and memories were a lane, I would walk right up to heaven and bring you back again" (author unknown).

On Easter Sunday, 2019, the light on top of the columbarium beckoned us into the memorial garden and the annual sunrise service. A crowd of people were gathered under an awning where they chatted, drank coffee, and enjoyed Dunkin' Donuts. The service was nondenominational, with the best of our local singers and a few talented guitar players. Everything felt right. After the plaque with his name and dates had been installed, we arranged to bring Joe there and held another service with a pastor. Now, our family name is there, and our son is in his final resting place.

It is 2023 as I write this, and I am happy Joe is close to places where people go; it's easy to say hello when I drive by or to stop to see his place (and our future place). Other families in the columbarium leave notes or trinkets for their loved ones. At Christmas, I left something too. It may sound depressing, but it's not. In fact, it is a nice place to be still for a moment and listen to the sounds of the wind in the trees.

3 Grief Counseling

In 2019, just six weeks after Joe's death, we went to Florida to meet our closest friends for a vacation we had planned a year earlier. Jim's brother and sister-in-law were also there, but I was not mentally present. We tried grief counseling in Florida, but the "workbook" didn't work for us. I was miserable being away from our daughters and grandchildren, and I was still consumed with the thought that our son might have been murdered. I was in an altered state the whole time.

Joe's death had exploded like a bomb inside our family. We were all wounded, our family circle was demolished, and we were disconnected from the people we were born to be with. In a way, it felt like we faced extinction.

When we came back from Florida, I found a counselor who met with all of us, including our teenaged grandchildren, and we shared each other's pain. Being together without Joe, we were off balance, like a body without all its appendages. We each missed something different about him and had our own reaction to what he did, but we all loved Joe. And we still do.

Initially, we talked to the counselor as a group so our grandchildren could feel free to express themselves with all of us and would know we valued their opinions and reactions as much as our own. Afterward, Jim and I went several more times.

I have spent the last few years trying to make sense of my son and trying to replicate the chronology of the unimaginable. From the beginning, we always thought that Joe could have changed his circumstances by taking any job where the employer was legally required to provide health insurance (then quitting after he found something he liked better), or if not that, he could simply have made a phone call to us. We would have been upset about the mess he was in, but we would have helped. We always did.

Joe's forwarded mail included two paychecks. If they had arrived before Christmas, they might have solved his immediate problem. What broke our hearts was that it would not have taken a lot of money to change his situation.

On one of our visits, our therapist asked us how we felt about guilt, since we had both mentioned it. She started by reading a definition that described guilt as an emotion resulting from a desire to hurt someone. We talked about it and agreed it is a feeling we have, not because we ever wanted to hurt Joe, but because we could have changed our reactions to his actions, and that in turn might have changed his response.

Joe was at his nadir, and counselors say change happens at the bottom, but I have learned that people who have a plan to end their lives are not easily diverted or convinced to accept treatment that would alter that future. I wish someone had intervened with our son . . . and I wish I had known enough to try. I think about that a lot, now that it is too late to do anything.

I think Joe thought we knew how bad things were because it was so obvious. I also think he was too proud to tell us on his own. He did not recognize the strength of our denial, and we did not consider the tremendous weight of the accumulation of failures that plagued him. He had lost his health, his job, his energy, and his car. He was on the list to be evicted, and he was probably in constant physical pain, and then, when he asked if he could come home, I said no.

I was bothered by my dream, and I wondered if the little voice that had asked, "Unto death?" was Joe. However, every time I fell apart, the same verse—"Trust in the LORD with all your heart and lean not on your own understanding"—calmed my mind. I wanted therapy because I needed it. When I felt like I was finished with professional help, I asked Lisa, the therapist, if she agreed, and she did.

But "finished" did not mean "over it" and, to be honest, I have no desire to be finished or over it. I am not reluctant to visit the topic of Joe—in fact, I think about him a lot. He still makes me sad, he still makes me laugh, and I love him more now than ever before, because now that I know more about him, I understand him better.

I'm sorry I told him that coming home wasn't the right thing to do. We had a contract with a life-care facility where we were building a new home for ourselves. We were about to put our home on the market, and having an adult son there at the time didn't seem wise.

Joe didn't say, "I only need a temporary place to stay, maybe for a couple of months," which was probably what he wanted and probably what I needed to hear.

And I didn't say, "Even in the new place we're building, there's room for you," which was true and maybe what he needed to hear. Neither did I say, "Even if we die, you can stay there, and if you need care, you'll be cared for," which was also true.

Every day for the rest of my life, I will wonder why I didn't say what he might have needed to hear. "Come home."

I did ask him to come home for Christmas, but he said, "No," so fast I could hear the door slam in his mind. It was already too late to make peace, and I understand why. It would have required him to reopen the wound of my rejection. There's no way he would've done that. I know.

As his mother, I needed to step up and provide grace and forgiveness. There are no circumstances that should cause a mom to withhold her parental love from a child. We learn that from Christ and the way he forgives us. When Jesus was asked to identify the greatest commandment, he condensed ten to two, and told us to love God and put him first in our lives. The second commandment can be loosely stated as "Do unto others as you would have them do unto you." We know it as the Golden Rule—and that's the one I broke when I told Joe not to come home.

4 The Police Report

On March 12, 2019, the official police report finally arrived from the Las Vegas Metropolitan Police Department. It included an administrative section listing the date, time, and officers on the scene. It was Saturday, December 28, 2018, at 10:55 A.M. There were seven names, including one supervisor and a crime scene analyst. There was a synopsis:

> *Dispatch received a call from the deceased subject's cell phone saying there had been a shooting in his apartment and to send the police quickly. The caller then hung up. Dispatch tried recalling the subject's phone multiple times, but it went directly to voicemail. [A] check of the cell phone revealed that the phone had called from the deceased's apartment.*

Under the Investigation section:

> *Officers arrived and made contact with management in the front office to gather information on the owner of the apartment. The owner of the apartment and the person who called dispatch were the same. According to [apartment] management, they had recently filed an eviction on him, but he had not been locked out yet. Officers were able to contact his emergency contact person, his mother in North Carolina. She stated he had been having some financial struggles lately but she had talked to him a few days earlier and he seemed fine. She also stated she had sent him some money for his birthday and Christmas. She asked if we would check on his welfare and call her back.*

The deceased's cell phone was left open, and the laptop was plugged in and sitting on the dining room table. The deceased's ID and car keys were sitting on the counter near the dining area.

We learned that Joe was neatly dressed in a long-sleeved, gray dress shirt, navy blue shorts, and white sneakers. He was sitting on his couch and had died from a self-inflicted gunshot wound. The apartment was neat. His laundry was freshly washed; it was still in the machine.

The police report answered questions we hadn't thought to ask, and it began to put my mind to rest about one thing. The dress shirt (I can see it in its plastic bag from the dry cleaner's), the trash (bagged and ready to go), the navy shorts, the phone and computer unlocked—none of those things seemed like a violent murder scene. In fact, it seemed more like a planned event than a crime.

The coroner had pronounced the time of death as December 29, 2018, at 1:40 P.M. We questioned the accuracy of the report because the police had called us earlier than that, but we were told that the time of death is always the time when the coroner turns in the written report. The report did not include the toxicology report or the 911 call since they are not handled through the police department. Those items would not arrive until later, after a legal request.

During my years in real estate, I wrote notes on my folder during complex negotiations so that I would have a record of details that might get lost. In the middle of this crisis, I took notes, and asked my girls to keep notes to establish a timeline that I could look at when things calmed down. I knew that someday I would want to mentally recreate "The Day Joe Died." But I not only lost the notes, I lost all memory of their existence. When they reappeared almost two years later, they were like scraps of debris on the ground after a tornado, pure gibberish.

No one told me that grief affects your memory, but one day I noticed the report of my visit to urgent care under a turtle magnet on the side of my refrigerator. It was then that I remembered and tried to understand my strange dream. As I prayed that night, I had not said, "Please, God, tell me what to do about Joe." I did not request strength or the words that would bring him home.

Instead, when I didn't know what to do, I promised God I would not second-guess what *He* decided to do. I thought I was doing the right thing.

***

We knew Joe had money problems—he had for years—but he dismissed discussion of it and never gave us any details. Our entire family used the same bank, and although we were no longer joint-owners with our children, they still used the accounts we'd set up for them when they were young. That made it easy for Joe to text or make a phone call and ask me to transfer money into his account. Since I knew his finances were shaky, I refrained from asking why he needed it. I didn't tell him he'd have to pay me back either, because when I did, he always said, "I'm not able to pay you back. If it's a loan, don't give it to me."

Questions created a chasm between us, and I was afraid if I pursued the answers, I'd lose contact with him altogether. Unfortunately, during the last year of his life, there was a problem between Joe and the bank. In April 2018, I made a generous deposit into his account, thinking that would cover whatever he needed, but the teller said, "His balance is still negative." I had never received any such information before, but I was not an account owner, so I assumed the teller had made a mistake.

When I told Joe about my deposit, he said, "That money is gone. Why did you make a deposit without asking me where to put it?"

Where else would I put it? I wondered, but aloud I said, "I don't understand where the money went." It didn't occur to me that his account might be so far in the negative that my deposit wouldn't cover the deficit.

I didn't argue with Joe, and I still don't know how he resolved his problem, but the next day he told me the bank had returned a portion of the deposit to my account, and he couldn't get them to do anything more. He didn't mention how much money he needed or the problem he was facing. He said he had moved to a new bank because they gave him a better deal. From that time until he died, we mailed him a check when he asked for money. He never complained, but I'm sure it was inconvenient compared to the instant transfers of the past.

Eventually, I asked Joe what had been going on when we had the bank problem. He said there had been no problem, it was all in my imagination. I said, "You mean you didn't get mad at me for putting money in the wrong account? None of that happened?"

"No," he said. "That was all in your head; you made it up."

I had to stop to think. I had recently suffered a bad fall, but I hadn't mentioned it to him. I had been experiencing some short-term memory lapses as well, which terrified me, but I had not let anyone know how bad they were.

Joe's response now made me afraid that I no longer knew what was real. The possibility that my memory was unreliable shook me to the core. I was silent for a long time.

After a while, Joe asked, "Why aren't you talking?"

"I have no words."

"You have words," he replied. "You're a writer—you always have words."

But I couldn't get any to form; all I could think about was the possibility that I had imagined our argument. There was another long pause before I said, "I don't know what to say."

"Well"—I could practically see his shrug—"if you can't talk, I'm not hanging on to an empty phone line. Goodbye."

Earlier in the month, Joe's sister and her family had gone to Las Vegas for a week's vacation and had hoped to spend some time with him, but he was not available. Finally, on their last day, just a few miles from his address, they called from their car to see if they could stop to see him. Joe emphatically told them no; he didn't feel well.

We had always tried to support him through his difficulties without enabling whatever it was that made dealing with him so difficult. We had no control over Joe, and he never gave us the benefit of knowing all the information about his situation. I sought help a number of times but was advised to stop overfunctioning.

Jim had a saying: "Don't ask how much the bill is unless you're going to pay it." Joe never told us how big the bill was, and he guarded his privacy fiercely. We didn't press him because he didn't want our opinions. On the other hand, we didn't want to understand his financial issues because we didn't want to own them.

As I write this, I am stunned that it didn't occur to me that he might have had debilitating clinical depression in addition to the multiple myeloma that was threatening him again. Instead of being sympathetic, I was angry and disappointed that he couldn't get his act together.

5 THE PHONE

On March 13, 2019, a day after receiving the police report, we received some of Joe's belongings, including his phone. Once Tammy and Jennifer figured out how to open it, we found a treasure trove of pictures we had never seen. I opened the Uber app and found a record of every trip he had taken after his car was repossessed on December twentieth. On the twenty-eighth, he was dropped off at a gun store and later picked up. On the same date, there was a gun purchase on his bank card statement.

David (Joe's friend and former boss), doesn't drink, so he hadn't spent time at the Gin Mill, but he knew Joe had friends there, and he contacted several of them for us. We spoke at length with a man and a woman who had been there with Joe until 3:00 or 4:00 A.M. on the twenty-ninth. Joe had told them he was feeling the way he had when his multiple myeloma was first diagnosed, and he thought it had returned. Looking back, they said their only clue that something might have been wrong occurred as they left the bar. Joe had tossed a new pack of cigarettes to the bartender and said, "Here, you can have these. I won't need them anymore."

They just thought he'd decided to quit smoking.

Instead of putting Joe's phone away, I kept it charged and began to look at it occasionally. I read years of texts between us. On December 20, 2018, there was a text from Joe: *"Can you send $300 to Walmart for me? Need it if you can."*

The text prompted me to remember the moment after dinner when the phone and the doorbell rang simultaneously. I was already fussy because I was preparing for a colonoscopy the next morning, and I urgently needed to get to the restroom, but our daughter and her family came in the front door like a flash mob. There were already several friends in the foyer, and someone handed me the phone. It was Joe calling about the money I needed to send him.

I was too overwhelmed by my immediate situation to say what I should have, which was, "I can't talk now! I have a serious emergency going on here. I'm preparing for a medical procedure, and the unintended consequences of your call and this crowd blocking the hall to my bathroom are going to be horrible." But I didn't. Instead, I quickly complained that banks would be closed over the holidays and I wanted to check the quickest, least expensive way to send the money.

"Check with Walmart," Joe suggested. I don't know why I hadn't thought of that immediately. Sending through Walmart was simple, and all he needed to receive the money was to show up with identification. It was almost as easy as being members of the same bank.

But I was too annoyed to be polite. "I've got my hands full here; why don't *you* call and check?" Then without waiting for a response, I gave the phone to someone and rushed into my bedroom.

As I pulled my bedroom door shut, my socks slipped on the wood floor, and I fell hard. My forehead hit the corner of my bureau, and I landed with my head under the chair. A big knot grew on my forehead, my eye instantly swelled almost shut, and the side of my face started to grow and change color. I looked like I'd been mugged. I will not say anything about the prep, except I was in awful shape.

When anything happens to me, I have to call my heart transplant hospital in Washington, D.C. I forgot all about Joe while Jim took me to the emergency room and I called my transplant team.

Our local hospital is connected to a medical school, and five resident doctors took turns interviewing Jim and me separately to make sure this had been an accident. They discussed the value of a CT scan versus the amount of radiation I would receive, and the potential damage to my kidneys from the radioactive dye. In the end, they all came to the same conclusion: I didn't need the scan because

I was completely lucid and had not lost consciousness. I'm sure every student in the building practiced the interview process with me.

The transplant nurse coordinator from D.C. didn't return my call until I was finally back home and in bed. It was after midnight and I was exhausted, but she insisted I go back to the ER and have the CT scan anyway. I just couldn't do it. I have no idea why I chose that particular time to become difficult; it is the only time I've ever refused to follow a doctor's orders. I was afraid I was going to be in trouble with all of my medical team. I was not acting like myself.

At 7:30 A.M. with a big swollen eye, a lump on my forehead, and the whole side of my face black and blue, I showed up at the endoscopy building. The nurses conferred with the doctor, and they all agreed that I could not have the colonoscopy.

At the end of my patience after the prep, the fall, and the emergency room visit, I refused to accept their decision. I had a major meltdown, even going so far as to demand that they call someone I thought was in charge of them. They looked at each other and said, "Who is that?" I had insisted they call a friend of ours who works in administration at a different hospital. I was so far out of line, I didn't know what to do with myself.

I asked them to let Jim come into the cubicle where I was, and my behavior got him all torqued up. They finally convinced us to go home. I agreed to fast for another day, drink another gallon of prep, and come back in the morning. As we left, in a nasty voice loud enough for everyone to hear, I said to Jim, "Let's agree to whatever they say and do nothing."

I left the gallon of prep in the garage and went to my grandson's birthday dinner, where I ate a piece of cake. I was awful. We got home, and I found another text from Joe. "*It costs $21 to send money instantly through Walmart. A wire from your bank costs $25. You can use your debit card to send it through Walmart. You can transfer up to $6,000. That $21 is the cost to send $1,000. Fees vary based on amount.*"

I didn't and still don't have a debit card. I had no idea why he mentioned $6,000; now I wonder if that is how much he needed to set things straight. I didn't know the mess he was in, and he didn't know I was so deep in my own mess that I didn't care about his mess.

I called him and started to tell him that I had fallen down and had houseguests and I hadn't had time to send the money. He stopped me immediately.

"What? You fell down? Are you okay? Did you hurt yourself?"

I brushed his concern aside. "Never mind about that. I'm okay. I'm going to Walmart now."

He knew his Christmas present was in the mail and I had sent it early because holiday mail is slow. When I told him it was a check for $1,000 and I had mailed it a week ago, he was so quiet I wondered if we were still connected.

"Are you there?" I asked.

"Yeah, I'm thinking," he answered.

"Thinking what?"

"If it's enough."

I was puzzled. I wondered what it would be enough for, but again, I didn't ask.

After a minute, he said, "Could you send it all through Walmart?" Then he repeated the request several times until I agreed, just to shut him up. I didn't like the idea, but I didn't have the heart to ask him to destroy the check already in the mail when it arrived. On the other hand, I didn't want to double his gift because then I would feel obligated to double the girls' gifts too.

But I was stupid. I should have sent a huge check or a larger amount through Walmart or jumped on a plane to Las Vegas with a pile of money in my purse. Those options actually ran through my mind as Jim and I drove to Walmart, but I thought Joe was a gambling addict. I didn't want him blowing it all at a casino and ending up alone without a dime and without any gifts on Christmas.

Now that he's gone, I think, "So what if he'd spent every cent before the holiday? It was his choice, his right to celebrate any way he wanted." I wanted him to have something separate for each of his big days, but I was being ridiculous; he didn't have big days. He was broke and miserable . . . and that's what he was every day.

He expected me to send all the money, but on the way to Walmart, I changed my mind. I have no idea why, but I sent only $350 for his birthday. I expected him to be furious, to call me and tell me so. But he was silent. I felt awful, so I took some medicine and went to bed.

The Walmart transfer went through. The check arrived and cleared the bank. As far as I knew, he had the money he needed.

But now I know how my son used his Christmas money. His bank statement listed it clearly: "Purchase of a gun, December 28, 2018." With that accomplished, he went out with friends and drank and sang karaoke till 3:00 A.M. (I have a video.)

And at 10:55 the next morning, Joe used the gun.

6 Regrets

It was April 17, 2019—four months after Joe's death—and all I could think about was how defeated my boy must have felt. From the beginning, his multiple myeloma diagnosis had cast a dark shadow over his future. I'm sure there were times when all he could think about was the pain, bone fractures, blood clots, and strokes that he was likely to experience on his way to immobility, more chemotherapy, unemployment, financial disaster, and the impossibility of living independently.

It's a wonder he kept going as long as he did.

His diagnosis should have qualified him for Social Security Disability benefits, but Joe never mentioned it, and we didn't either. I was told it could take a lawyer up to three years to get approval for a small amount like $1,000 per month. In addition, the eligibility rules are so restrictive that they discourage recipients from earning any extra money independently, despite the fact that staying engaged in life is the best thing someone with a disabling disease can and should do to help fight depression, and encourage feelings of self-worth.

The cancer clinic had harvested enough stem cells for a second transplant, but if his cancer had come back, as he apparently thought it had, it's unlikely that he would have been approved for another transplant. Joe had no insurance, and he was not a careful steward of his health. Unlike most men his age, he must have felt terrible every day. Joe's scans revealed the fragile bones of an old man. His problems were exacerbated by morbid obesity, a disease that leads to lack of mobility and depression, which only compounded everything else he was dealing with.

When I look at our pictures of my son, I see a very sad man. But the pictures David sent from a box in Joe's apartment show a happy Joe—skiing and fishing and mountain climbing and traveling with people we did not know in places we did not recognize. There are photos of Joe on beaches and in crowded bars where everyone was drinking and singing.

We hardly remember happy-go-lucky Joe, but there was a time when he radiated happiness. He was so healthy, he sometimes rode his bike to work. But after he decided to work nights, his activities changed. Now I wish he'd had even more fun. I'm sorry we disapproved of his lifestyle, and I wish we had all made different decisions along the way.

I was awful, and I have no excuse. I thought I was a Christian, but my behavior refutes that. I was more like the Pharisees who infuriated Jesus with their manmade laws and preposterous rules.

I spent years worrying that something would happen to Joe and we wouldn't know anything about it or have a way to help him—and yet, when I saw the shocking state he was in, I did nothing. It didn't occur to me that what I feared had already happened.

I can't fathom how we went on without question. We were busy and we stayed busy; that was our excuse for everything. We kept going, one step after another, into the quagmire. We didn't think he would lie—he wasn't a liar. And he didn't lie. He was a merciful misleader who simply chose not to relay the parts of the truth that would disturb us. He committed the sin of omission.

Did we lie? Only to ourselves when we refused to see the truth. And, well, yes. We lied to him by having expectations based on options he didn't have. We must have added to his problems with our disappointment. I wish we had known better and had done better.

I remind myself of Nancy Reagan, who solved the drug problem with the advice, "Just say no." Some problems have more tentacles than Medusa had snakes on her head. "Yes or no," "black or white," and "all or nothing"—these are not solutions to the problems parents have in relationships with their adult children.

I did not recognize my contribution to the dynamic we struggled with, and I didn't realize the only person I could fix was the one I saw in my own mirror, the one I could barely handle myself. Sometimes one person's changes can affect another, and sometimes they do not.

Since Joe's death, I have had to examine my flaws and imperfections in the harsh light of truth. My only choice has been to accept forgiveness from the God who forgives us all, and to move forward with love and the same forgiveness I have received from above. It is not easy, and I definitely fall short daily, but it is something I strive for. The battle is ongoing.

The only thing I can do now is speak my truth; if my candor rings a bell in your heart and prevents you from repeating my mistakes, then I have achieved my goal. I don't want anyone to do what I did. I don't want you to ruin your relationship with your child or your parent.

We all have bad in us, and we are all works in progress. I am not the same person I was before I gave my life to Christ on September 3, 2011. That's the day I received two hearts—a physical one from my beautiful donor, Shelly, and a spiritual one from God, who made me whole. I'm better now, but I am human and I will never be perfect. That I speak freely of my failure is required by my definition of repentance.

This is my confession; it would be of no use to anyone if I said it in a dark closet to someone who kept it a secret. I have no choice but to share the most important lesson of my life with other people who might find something in my ramblings that will prevent them from making similar mistakes. This is how the truth can set you free, and it is my example of how God uses bad for good. I pray to be used in that way. It is all I have to give you, and it is all I can do for Joe.

7 Remembering Joe

On May 1, 2019, I started gathering pictures of Joe to take to the memorial we were planning at the Vienna Inn, everyone's favorite bar in our town. It's a landmark—the town council used to meet there, and all the kids' ball teams stopped there on Saturdays after their games. These days, the cook has been to culinary school, but the rest of the place is just as it was in the old days, and the hot dogs are still famous.

On the fifth of May, from 6:00 to 9:00 P.M., we had it all to ourselves for a celebration of Joe's life. About sixty people came. His friend, Mike, came from Texas with his mother. His Villanova fraternity brothers came from New York, Connecticut, New Jersey, and Pennsylvania. His Aunt Anne and cousin Rose came from Pennsylvania. His friend, Marsha, came from Colorado, and his sisters, Tammy and Jennifer, along with a bunch of other friends who all loved him, were there. We played music from his phone nonstop on the jukebox. The bar was open, the food was great, and we had pictures of Joe on the TV screens.

Joe would have loved his party. We had a book for friends to sign and leave memories. His friends in Las Vegas had already had two parties for him, and in Colorado, they'd had a poker game in his honor on St. Patrick's Day and donated the pot to the Shelly Whitman Scholarship for the child of an organ donor. (Shelly Whitman was my heart donor, and the proceeds from my book about that experience help the child of an organ donor at East Carolina University, our local college.)

I started the memories by talking about Joe's DUI on a bicycle when he and his friend John, who were both in middle school, snuck into our liquor in the middle of the night and then decided to ride their bikes into town. Jim and I were peacefully asleep in our home when the local police called. The boys had fallen off their bikes into the hedges a block from our house, and the police had taken them to the station and put them in a cell.

Jim got up and went to the station house to retrieve them. When he got there, they had thrown up in the cell. The police gave them paper towels, and Jim waited while they cleaned up their mess. We had a major fit and vowed they could never play together again. We actually thought that being sick would teach them not to drink alcohol. We were fools.

Jennifer, Tammy, and Jim called for people to come and speak. Tom, a straight-laced honor student before he became Joe's big brother in his fraternity, talked about what Joe had done at his wedding. As best man, Joe had fifty keys made and secretly passed them out at the reception. He included family members, friends of all ages, and even the nuns who were like family. After his toast to the bride and groom, Joe asked the ladies who still had a key to Tom's apartment to bring them up. A crowd of women waving keys rushed forward. I think I even remember one as old as I am now, with a walker, but I am not sure. It remains the funniest thing I have ever seen at a wedding.

His friend, Mike, said Joe had done the same thing the following year when he was best man for him in Texas. He said he'd thought Joe was only his Joe, and he was surprised to see that he belonged to so many other people.

Every year, Joe had gone to Mike's house first thing on Christmas morning to open gifts and have breakfast with Mike and his mom and sister, while we waited for both boys to come to our house so we could open our gifts and have breakfast. Even after Mike moved to Texas, Joe continued the tradition. Mike's mom held a very special place in Joe's heart, and when he graduated from Villanova, she gave him a flag flown over the U.S. Capitol in honor of the event.

It was therapeutic to listen to stories from friends who'd thought highly of Joe. Jennifer's friend, Withers, talked about how honored she and their girl gang had felt when he went out with them after they graduated from college.

At the party, I learned that Joe and his fraternity brothers used to go to Atlantic City and gamble until they had no money left. In the car afterward, they'd empty their pockets to gather coins for tolls. One night after combining their change, they were still too short to make it back to school. Joe said, "I guess we can stay at my house." They were shocked to find they were only minutes from a place to crash. After that, they gambled, stayed at our beach house, got up early, and rushed back to campus before anyone realized they had been gone. We had no knowledge of this.

Joe's fraternity brother, Pete, spoke about their mutual love of poetry, in particular "The Love Song of J. Alfred Prufrock," by T. S. Eliot. Once he had recited the first stanza by heart, and Joe had continued from where he stopped. When Pete was in the Peace Corps, they had toured eastern Europe together. Pete finished his story by reciting "A Piece of the Storm," a beautiful poem by Mark Strand, a Pulitzer prize-winning poet laureate, in Joe's honor.

The Villanova crowd and our family moved to the bar at the Hyatt Regency in Tysons Corner after the party ended. There, several of Joe's friends reported a moment when they had felt his presence. His friend, Bill, asked me if I had experienced that. I had not.

"You will," he said, "and when you do, you'll know it's him."

In Joe's name, his Villanova friends sponsored a student who studied in Ireland that summer, and we attended the wonderful presentation/reception by the Villanova Center for Irish Studies at the Grace Kelly residence in Philadelphia.

***

If there is a storeroom in our brains where all the sights we have ever seen and all the conversations we have ever had are organized in file cabinets for our eternal retrieval, Joe's death was an earthquake that knocked over my cabinets and spilled parts of conversations and pictures of events into such disarray that a master quilter couldn't have pieced them together with even a hint of their former pattern.

Initially, I was lost in my thoughts, lost in my room, and lost in my head. Being anxious was not helpful; I had to wait for the ground to settle. Writing helped me capture the moments in my mind, but putting them together in a sensible order has not been easy. I find the ground continues to shift. For a while I couldn't write because I was in such mental chaos. Frustrated, I bought Dragon Speech Recognition software, a program that transcribes voice to print, and I recorded myself the way doctors do when making notes on patients' charts. When I listened back, however, I often couldn't recognize my own voice, and the transcriptions were largely incoherent.

Now that I've found a semblance of order, I've organized my memories to keep them alive. Joe is deeply missed. I don't want to forget the moments we had with our son who left us without discussion or goodbye. An Irish exit.

But there is unfinished business between us, and it makes me sad because if we'd have had a real conversation, I believe we might have been able to stop him. It would have been uncomfortable and difficult for Joe to be vulnerable, but it's also hard to kill yourself.

And there I go, bargaining. It is almost impossible to get past that stage of grief. But as I go back to it, God reminds me to trust Him and lean not on my own understanding.

Jim and I must have been difficult for Joe to be around because we are happy people. Joe had forgotten how to be happy. Even his remission from multiple myeloma had not given him more than a short rush of euphoria. Then he was right back in the same position with a nightmare's worth of credit card debt and job changes that took him to better situations but only temporarily; none lasted more than a year.

Instead of using a standard wallet, Joe had a credit card holder jammed with a gazillion cards. After he died, I requested his credit card records to see if they would provide evidence of his gambling. The few cards that were up to date had very low limits that he regularly exceeded. His minimum payments did not help because the penalties and interest finance charges were outrageous. His debt multiplied faster than rabbits on hormones.

8 In the Beginning

I remember Joe's first day of preschool in California. Tammy, his older sister, had hopped out of the car and happily waved goodbye. Joe, however, jumped over the seat and wrapped himself around the steering wheel. I ordered, pleaded, and cajoled, but he just held on tighter and cried louder. I remembered stories about my father who was so stubborn as a child that he held his breath until he passed out if he didn't get his way. The battle with Joe was futile; I finally agreed that he didn't have to go to school that day.

He spent a week holding on to the steering wheel before I gave up and kept him home for another year. He was a December baby so it wasn't a problem, but I couldn't figure it out—he was capable, intelligent, and easy to get along with, why wouldn't he go to school? The next year, he had no hesitation.

As a toddler, Joe had often suffered respiratory problems from allergies and asthma. Still, he was quick to read, bright, and inquisitive. Although we were told to limit his physical activity, he threw himself into imminent danger at every opportunity. He must have felt frustrated because he was not allowed to be as active as other kids. He loved *Mister Rogers' Neighborhood* and *Wild Kingdom* on TV and anything with wheels that went fast enough to throw him into the air when it crashed. He invented a game where he lined a hallway with pillows, laid down on the floor, bent his legs, and convinced his younger sister to sit on his feet while he catapulted her "to the moon." It was so much fun that she cried when he got in trouble for doing it.

An eager student in elementary school, he excelled at everything. When we moved closer to town, and his school changed, his friends changed, and so did his behavior. He was suddenly Wile E. Coyote.

Once Jim wanted Joe to move a pile of rocks so that we could plant some flowers in our new yard. He gave Joe a pail and offered him twenty-five cents each time he filled it. Instead of picking ordinary rocks, Joe picked rocks so large that one or two filled the whole pail. Jim complained, and Joe passionately defended his right to select his own rocks. Jim used to refer to him as a "sea lawyer," because he was so skilled at avoiding things he didn't want to do.

Although he was not motivated to perform at his new school, he was very entrepreneurial. This school had a snack store where the children had a limited opportunity to buy treats. Joe almost put the store out of business by selling gum by the slice, in competition with the more expensive packs sold at the store. When we were called about this, we punished Joe by restricting him to his room. That seemed okay with him. He pretended he was doing homework and read all night long. We talked to him about a boarding school; he said he would run away, and we believed him. I sometimes wonder if he was smoking pot with his new friends. Even if he finished his assignments, he "forgot" to turn them in. He did not do well unless he liked his teacher, and that did not happen often. Still, he did beautifully on standardized tests.

The day he passed the test for his driver's license, he was stopped going ninety-six miles an hour on the Dulles toll road. The policeman noted that he was still accelerating (in an old blue car of mine that had never been over sixty miles an hour). Joe left his ticket and the car keys on his dad's desk for Jim to find in the morning. Speeding on the toll road was a federal offense. Everything about it was a big deal, including federal court in Alexandria.

The fact that Joe had been with his friend Andrew sent me over the edge. A few years earlier, Andrew's older brother had died in an accident, and I couldn't get over the fact that Joe drove recklessly with him in the car. I insisted that Joe go to Andrew's house and apologize to his mother.

After that we had World War Three about the dress code in court. I knew that Jim would be dressed in a suit for work, and at that time people in real estate dressed up, so I would be wearing a suit too.

But our son had just had a growth spurt and had no dress-up clothes that fit. He refused to go shopping, and his standard attire was shorts or jeans and T-shirts. We went round and round about it, but he did his thing. When Joe's case was called in court, the judge was furious.

"What are you doing in my courtroom dressed like that?" he demanded. "Where did you think you were going today? Your parents knew where they were going; why didn't you?"

Joe was ordered to pay a fine with money he earned himself, but that didn't change his driving habits. He was always Evel Knievel behind the wheel of a vehicle, and he never stopped hating dress-up clothes.

He spent a lot of time lost in books about military history, Dungeons and Dragons, fantasy, mythology, astrology, and all things dark and mysterious. In the summer before his junior year in high school, he came to me and said he wanted to quit school. I was dumbfounded. He asked for one of my big real estate map books of the whole area around Washington, D.C. He had already applied and been accepted for a job as a messenger.

Without making a big deal of it, I gave him the map book and let him try. He spent two days on the road, mostly in traffic, according to him. He was so frazzled after hours of gridlock on the Beltway, I-95, and the "mixing bowl" of roads, that he quit work rather than get on the Beltway and drive to Springfield to pick up what would have been his first paycheck.

That did not discourage him, however. Instead, without telling us, he got a job at a call center that was a short bike ride from our house. We noticed that he was in a good mood and seemed to be doing well, so we breathed a sigh of relief. He didn't tell us about that job until he had to ask permission to work nights so he could make more money. He was selling vacation lots, and he was the best salesperson in the office. He was even going to get a bonus.

We were stunned. We wanted him to do homework not sales pitches. He wanted to quit school again, and we were tearing our hair out. We made him quit that job, but his talent on the telephone was not to be denied. No wonder he was drawn to the idea of owning his own call center later in life.

By the time he was a senior in high school, it was almost impossible to get him up and out the door. At the end of the year, I was told he had accumulated forty-four excused late arrivals since Christmas. All I can say is, I did my best. Joe had all the requirements to graduate, and he did graduate, but he was not allowed to walk with his graduating class because he had not turned his work in on time. Jim and I went to the school and spoke to someone who had no sympathy at all. If we knew then what we know now, we wouldn't have tried to defend him against a teacher. He needed boundaries, not excuses.

The interesting thing is that, based on his performance, Joe had been kept in the lowest English section through high school. He didn't participate, didn't turn in assignments, and sat in the back of the room with his textbook open in front of him and the book he was reading inside the textbook. He did very well on tests, however, and his SAT scores were excellent. He spent a year in community college where he was a straight-A student, then applied to Villanova without first mentioning it to us. To say we were shocked is an understatement. When he was accepted by Villanova as a sophomore, we were thrilled.

When he was a senior in college, we expected him to be anxious to get a job. After all, he was the kid who couldn't wait to be finished with high school in order to work as a messenger, a vacation-lot salesman, a tinker, a tailor, or candlestick maker. But Joe did not seem to know what he wanted to do with his life.

One thing was certain, though, from the time he learned to read, which happened before school began; he was the most prolific reader I have ever encountered. He loved books and he read in color. No matter how sick he was, no matter if it was the end of his days, he was reading all the time, on all sorts of subjects, including poetry. When he began to speak, he sometimes spoke in rhyme.

After a job fair at Villanova, he told us that the only interesting job was teaching in an inner-city school for troubled kids. It probably would have been great for him, but that didn't occur to him or to us. He shrugged and said, "I just can't see myself wearing a suit and carrying a briefcase every day."

Jim and I worked hard to keep our opinions to ourselves as we waited for him to come up with a plan for the future. Instead, he moved back home about three weeks before graduation, telling us that he'd decided to withdraw to protect his GPA because the bookstore had run out of books for his Russian class, and it was better to withdraw than to flunk Russian when he was three credits shy of graduation. I was almost catatonic, especially when he wanted to wear his cap and gown, walk, and celebrate with all his friends and classmates!

I was dead set against a ceremony that didn't end with a degree in his hand. Jim told him he couldn't hang around the house without a job, so he worked at the local TGI Friday's restaurant, which seemed like half work and a lot of hanging out with friends.

I'm more understanding now. Obviously, he wasn't ready to grow up and choose a career. When I think about it now, he was always independent—he just wasn't self-supporting. Nor was he interested in doing what we wanted or expected.

I found an apartment for him near Villanova and leased it myself because no decent place would accept a young student as a tenant. Joe went to work at the Chart House restaurant while he took that last class. We were there to see him walk in 1991. We had a big party, and it was a wonderful time.

9 Leaving the Nest

After graduation, Joe and his girlfriend moved into a trendy new apartment near the waterfront in Philadelphia. He continued to work at the Chart House, where he learned a great deal about wine and played golf with his coworkers. I'm sure he was a terrific waiter. I can see him upselling fancy wines and raw clams to the customers with great regularity.

We were happy he had graduated from a good school, but now we expected him to do what other people's children did: use the degree he had to get a meaningful job or continue with his education. We didn't realize that he might not be ready for adulthood or a career yet.

Joe decided he needed a new car. He told me he wanted a used Honda like the one a friend had just found for $7,000. I was impressed with his good sense and thought I would like to help him. I gave him the money, all of it. Don't ask why; I don't know myself. But before I knew what had happened, he used the money I had given him as the down payment on a new Infiniti. He was so excited and proud of that car.

I was surprised but remained quiet, even when he found the car payments impossible and traded in the Infiniti for a tiny Honda Civic with payments he could afford. He had to fold himself down into a much smaller man to get into that car, but he jumped in with a jaunty wave and gunned the motor like it was a monster truck. That was pure Joe.

Jim started a small auto-financing company in 1993, and he asked Joe if he wanted to move back to Virginia to run it. He did, but visiting car dealers and negotiating and managing car loans didn't challenge him for long. He had trouble keeping the office open during business hours. I wanted him to use his spare time to get another degree; there were many good schools around, and we would have paid for him to attend. He had taken the prep course and the Law School Admission Test (LSAT); we thought he would make a great lawyer. He was born to win arguments; he did it with us all the time. But he didn't want to go to school anymore.

Life was peaceful until Jim, who had been traveling for about ten years without a word of complaint, stunned us by declaring he no longer wanted to get on an airplane every Monday morning to go work. The car business had grown large enough to interest Jim and he quit consulting to manage it. Joe was unhappy about losing his position at the bottom of the food chain.

We should have known better than to try to create synergy between a father and son who had always been polar opposites yet somehow exactly alike. If one said *black*, the other said *white*. Neither was ever wrong to my knowledge, and I didn't consider it a problem since I am never wrong either. They pushed each other's buttons, and they both pushed mine. With Joe I was a softy, and that annoyed his dad because I often undermined him by going behind his back.

Jim has always been a decision-maker—he declares, points, and insists. He's always thinking about a big picture and moving forward. In sales you would call it the "foot-in-the-door technique." His personal style can create a kerfuffle, but he immediately forgets about it because he's so focused on finishing what he starts. Any change of course happens after he has calmed down and reconsidered.

Joe, on the other hand, was a person who ruminated. He remembered everything, forever. He didn't seem to believe that starting something was a commitment to finishing it. Sorry to say, I can relate to that.

Stuck in the middle, I tried to run interference and didn't establish my own limits. Things never changed—I didn't step up, and

I couldn't control either of them. They were oil and water. They only occupied common ground when they discussed the basketball program of their alma mater, Villanova. In those moments, oil and water became peanut butter and jelly.

It didn't take us long to realize that Joe and his father couldn't work together; we did our best to make sure Joe received a generous severance. We didn't want him to ever feel cheated. I saw an article in the paper about lay-offs at AT&T: after thirteen years of service, the employee severance package included six months' salary and matching retirement contributions. In Jim's company, the retirement was 25 percent of salary. He decided to match the AT&T severance in hopes of keeping family harmony, even though Joe had only worked for him about eighteen months. But mixing business and family is a land mine in the best of circumstances.

When Joe left the car business, he went to Hoboken, New Jersey, to live with college friends who worked in New York City. It wasn't until his funeral that we found out he had gone to the wrong address when he was applying for a job in brokerage, but instead of redirecting him to where he was supposed to be, the supervisor there hired him. We also heard that he was Top Gun of his training class. Joe was funny in the way he kept his news (good and bad) to himself. Everything was top secret from us.

Being a stockbroker seemed to suit Joe, and he soon held all the stock-trading licenses. In an effort to build a book of clients, he went the extra mile. Once he called me from a train in Connecticut after he had personally delivered a check to a client at the end of a long day. The couple was so touched, they'd insisted he stay for dinner.

He was doing well and planning for the future, but he had a boss he compared to Nurse Ratched, who terrorized Jack Nicholson in *One Flew Over the Cuckoo's Nest*. When several of his coworkers left to work at another brokerage house, Joe was also recruited. He asked for my advice, and he was so unhappy, I encouraged him to go.

I was in real estate, where being recruited meant a bump in bonuses and an agreement from the new company to make up lost wages from the company-side of future commissions. Noncompete clauses didn't exist for me, and I'm sure I didn't advise him well. I don't really know what happened, but it didn't turn out well for Joe. One reason might have been his exit interview; he told me he'd been honest and that it might be a problem. Although the others from his office who were recruited were not fined, Joe told me he was.

He didn't explain, and he didn't complain. As the saying goes, "Your friends don't need an explanation, and your enemies wouldn't believe it." Joe was soon unemployed and taking a bus to Connecticut for a job he did enjoy—building elaborate decks and playgrounds with a friend from his brokerage job. He said he could have collected unemployment insurance, but he didn't believe in "sucking off the government."

No matter, Joe did not build decks for long. Soon he called from Hoboken to say he had accepted a brokerage job in Colorado because he had always wanted to live there.

He did? Who knew? Not us.

He said he was leaving almost immediately, and within a week, I had found an apartment for him that was close enough to ride his bike to work if he wanted, and sometimes he did. He loved Colorado.

He soon had a list of 14,000-foot peaks that he planned to climb; I think he did seven. He described leaving his apartment at 3:00 A.M. and starting the climb in the dark so that he and a few friends and their dog could reach the summit in full sun. We have pictures of beautiful scenery with people we don't know and a big black dog that went with them.

Once I was alone in my house in the middle of the night, and I heard him call, "Mom!" so loudly that I jumped up in bed. I thought he was in the room. It was weird. Later, we were on the phone, and I asked him where he had been the night before. He said he had been climbing a mountain and had almost fallen.

The first Christmas he was in Colorado, we rented a ski-in condo and took the whole family out to see him. It was definitely as beautiful as he said, and for someone who was a great skier, fisherman, hiker, and lover of outdoor adventures like whitewater rafting, Colorado was perfect. He told us about night skiing, where you park your car, jump over a guardrail and ski through the trees in the dark. I have no idea if that really happened, but in our experience, he was much more daredevil than we were comfortable knowing.

He had a busy social life; he played cards with a group from work, belonged to a gun club, and went hunting with a friend from the Midwest. He went scuba diving and even had me buy him his own oxygen tank so he wouldn't have to use one that might be unsafe when he did a really deep dive. He had spent the whole week when we were in Hawaii getting certified. When Jim traveled for work he earned a huge amount of hotel and airline rewards points. We were lucky to use them on family vacations.

Joe loved to travel. Once a friend of ours ran into him on a slope in Whistler, British Columbia, and called to tell us how happy he looked and what a great skier he was. Joe went fishing in Argentina with high school friends. Best of all, in my opinion, he had a wonderful girlfriend.

But in 2005, after working in Colorado for about five years, he called to say he wanted to move back to the East Coast. We were so excited about the prospect of spending time with him, we didn't ask many questions. He asked if he could stay in the attic apartment of our vacation home in Ocean City, New Jersey, which we rented separately from the rest of the house.

We agreed and immediately gave notice to our month-to-month tenant. We expected Joe to use our house as a base while he looked for a job in New York or nearby. We told him he could stay in the apartment rent-free, and I offered to fly out and help him move. He was adamantly against that. Around this time, he also told us he had taken a distribution from his IRA and miscalculated the taxes he owed. He needed $10,000 for taxes, and we sent it. None of this made sense, but we decided not to ask because it was more important to get him close enough to see him with regularity.

About three weeks before he was supposed to arrive, Jim and I discussed our fear that he might think we were okay with him living rent-free in the beach house forever. We discussed a lease with him; it would take effect six months after his arrival and cost $100 less than the previous tenant had paid. Joe was outraged. He said he had made plans that didn't include rent. We signed a lease agreement and sent it to him in the mail so that he would see that we were serious about him moving toward financial independence. He ignored the lease, and we ignored the fact that he ignored it. That was business as usual with us.

Months earlier, Joe had asked me to pay off his car. He pointed out that I had helped each of his sisters buy a house, and I had told him I would help him when he was ready. He said he didn't want a house, he wanted to get rid of his car payment. I said I would help him buy a house any time, but I didn't feel the same about a car. I was in real estate; I could sell my children a house and give them my commission. I was glad to help, but it wasn't like I could or would buy a house or car for anyone.

Suddenly, he told us he had sold his Toyota SUV and needed $1,500 to buy a car for the cross-country trip. It was another thing that didn't make sense, but I sent him that money too, and he set off. I'll never forget the huge dark wells of his eyes when he arrived. He looked like he hadn't slept in weeks.

While he was in Colorado, Joe had told us about a custom-made firearm he had purchased from a well-known gunmaker. It was an investment, he said, because the man was old and his life's work was increasing in value to collectors. He had even purchased a gun safe to protect it. He lived in a nice apartment, the one I found for him, and he had a cleaning lady. Yet when he arrived in New Jersey he was in a broken-down car, dressed like a hobo, and had almost nothing else with him. His appearance was so shocking, we didn't know what to think. It was as if he had lost everything he owned. Seeing him like that scared us. But we didn't focus on that.

I thought he would want to rest after his long trip, but he insisted on going to Atlantic City immediately. I suggested that once he'd rested, we could go shopping to buy a new couch for his empty apartment. He suggested instead that I just give him the money for the couch so he could shop later alone. I refused, and he complained that I didn't treat him the way I treated his sisters—I would have given them the money to shop when they felt like it. He was right, but I didn't care. I wanted to make sure I got a good deal on the couch, and I didn't want him to take my money and lose it playing poker.

In the end, he went to Atlantic City without my money, and I bought a couch that was delivered to the attic apartment that he didn't move into. He stayed in the main house for nine months before he finally moved upstairs to sit on his couch and start paying rent.

While it was frustrating and discouraging to know that Joe was struggling, I put it out of my mind because I couldn't go around the corner and see that his car was in the driveway instead of at a workplace. It was like sending a child to college; if the child doesn't show up for class or he spends his money on beer instead of books, you don't lose sleep about it because you don't see the consequences of his behavior or experience the aggravation of it in real time.

Distance made it easier for Joe to live the way he wanted because we couldn't drop in to check on him. There is no doubt that we would have dropped in, and there's no doubt that he would have perceived our sudden arrival as a negative event. With distance, we all had a diluted sense of normalcy. Opposing expectations make living together difficult for parents and children who have issues.

The same cognitive dissonance that makes relationships stressful exists in people with addictions like gambling. They talk about quitting, but for an addict, losing money is just a reason to play again for the chance to win their losses back. You can't win if you don't play.

I think Joe enjoyed working in the stock market partly because it was a socially acceptable way to gamble. At one point, I asked him to make the same moves in my retirement account as he did in his IRA, and I was shocked to see my money disappear faster than a rabbit in a magician's hat. I stopped gambling immediately.

Joe may have started gambling with his retirement account. Why else would he complain about how long it took to earn his IRA back after he lost it all trading puts and calls (a way to make money by anticipating the future price of a stock on a particular date).

We had assumed Joe was moving back East because he missed his family, and we had been happy about it. I vaguely remember him saying he was going to play poker, but I did not think that meant playing cards was going to be his job or his career! Now I wonder if we ever really heard what he said, especially if it was contrary to our world view.

10 Texas Hold'em

In the early 2000s, when only a few states had casinos, online poker sites like PokerStars and Party-Poker became extremely popular. The advertising used by these sites misled people into believing they were legitimate enterprises (i.e., regulated and licensed in the United States). They were not.

In 2003, an unknown young player named Chris Moneymaker won the World Series of Poker on TV after starting with an $86 online entry-fee. After he won the $2.5 million jackpot, Texas Hold'em and online gambling suddenly seemed legitimate. Soon it was a national pastime for college students, day traders, and our son, Joe.

The whole world seemed to be gambling. If it wasn't day trading in the stock market, it was poker online. I was not a fan, but despite the obvious clues in front of us, I didn't think our son was under its spell. Nor did I think it would ruin his future.

As a Realtor, I had clients who lived in lovely houses and were day traders. I had a friend whose son left a successful career on Wall Street to play Texas Hold'em. I heard parents complain about their children playing online poker instead of attending class and knew of another friend's teenage daughter who lost $800 playing poker online at a slumber party.

I wouldn't have said gambling seemed normal, but it was definitely a fad. I didn't think it could be a death sentence.

I now think Joe liquidated the IRA he had in the stock market to use as his stake to start gambling full time, and I think he lost it before he left Colorado. He kept his cards so close to his vest that we never knew what was going on, but it should have been obvious that his life was a total disaster when he arrived in Ocean City the way he did.

At one point, Joe said he had planned to pay his monthly expenses with the money he made from gambling online, but that income disappeared when online gambling became illegal. A lot of people lost a fortune when their assets were seized from the online poker sites. Now that I think I know what he was doing, I understand why Joe was always broke. I still don't understand why he gambled.

Recently, after reading about the poker boom of 2003–2006, and the crash after Congress passed the Unlawful Gaming Act of 2006, I realized what our son was caught up in. I had seen it; I had heard about it; I knew people whose lives were affected by it—*our own lives were affected by it!*—but I didn't connect the dots to us or to Joe while it was happening.

Months after his death, one of his friends called and talked to me about how things had fallen apart for him. That's when I learned that after five successful years in Colorado, Joe had started arriving late for work. He was the manager, and his team was worried about him. One time, when everyone was looking for him, a member of his team finally reached him on his cell phone.

"Where are you?" the coworker asked. "Is something wrong? You're supposed to be at work."

"No, I'm fine," Joe answered. "I'm at the casino; I can make more money here than I can at the office." The casino was about an hour away from work.

Puzzled, the coworker said, "Well, we didn't want to get you in trouble, but we were so worried, we were about to have the police go to your apartment to check on you. You'd better come in and talk to the boss."

Joe seemed surprised that anyone was looking for him. "Nothing's wrong," he said. "I've been doing well here."

After that, he met with his supervisor, who told him that he was well liked and had a great future with job security and a satisfying career if he chose to stay. Poker might be okay for the moment, but it was going to prove unsustainable over time. Instead of buckling down, however, Joe resigned from his job to become a professional gambler.

It was a relief to finally hear what happened from someone who knew him at that time.

Joe knew everything there was to know about money and money management. He was a trained financial planner; he held the licenses necessary to sell stocks; he could negotiate loans; he loved to strategize and plan—and yet he was a poor manager of his own money and resources. After his death, I saw a form he had filled out for a debt consolidation loan. His explanation for his financial predicament was simple: "I spend more than I make."

We spoke to him fairly often, but we didn't see the truth in living-color that self-destructed in front of us. One of our best friends said, "You didn't want to know." How true. I still don't want to know.

***

When Joe moved to Ocean City, New Jersey, his dad thought he needed reliable transportation to go on interviews and get a real job. Jim had an old Mercedes that he drove around town that was still in very nice shape, but rather than give it to Joe, he offered to sell it to him for $500, to be paid when he was able. Joe was not enthusiastic; he insisted he didn't want or need a car. But Jim had it all tuned up and detailed, and we took it to the Shore. Reluctantly, Joe accepted the car with its title. But before a month had passed, he called to say, "Do you want the car back? Because I really don't want it."

"Reliable transportation is good for you to have," Jim said. "Keep it."

Joe countered with, "Well, I need five hundred dollars right now. If you don't want the car back, I'm going to put it on Craigslist and sell it for that."

"Go ahead and sell it," Jim said. "You have the title; it's yours."

We never heard about the car again, and Joe didn't complain about taking the bus to Atlantic City or walking home from the bus station in the middle of the night. In fact, he said he enjoyed walking up the boardwalk in the cold. He stopped at Dunkin' Donuts on his way.

When Joe first arrived, we drove up to the Shore almost every other weekend to see how he was doing (and to see if he had done anything about finding a job). He dismissed our concerns about his gambling, and finally became so sick of hearing about it that he agreed to go to Baltimore with us to meet some people who treated that addiction. We told him that if these people said he was not addicted to gambling, we wouldn't mention it again.

The visit didn't take long. They interviewed the three of us separately and, at the end, told us that Joe likely did have an addiction, but his gambling, they said, would not change until he wanted it to change. The ride home was surreal. Joe was outraged that we could believe he had a problem, and he couldn't forgive us for subjecting him to the humiliation.

After that, if he knew we were coming to the Shore, he was gone by the time we arrived. If our arrival was a surprise, he left when he saw us and didn't come back. Sometimes, we saw him walk past our window without a glance or a wave. We stayed in our neutral corners and time passed.

I became convinced that living in our beach house made gambling so convenient that Joe would never get a normal job and leave. I was cured of buying cars for him until the day Jim's sister mentioned that she was buying a new car and the dealer would only pay $1,000 for her old Jeep. She asked if I wanted to buy it for Joe, and after checking with him, I did.

As I write this, my heart is heavy with the realization of how tough it was for our son. I spent so much time being miserable about him, it didn't occur to me that his life was much worse than my misery. Regardless of what occurred in Colorado, he did not succeed as a professional gambler in Atlantic City. Maybe the pressure of rent and regular costs of living ruined his luck. In any case, we never acknowledged gambling as a career, and we kept praying for him to get an ordinary job.

Jim asked me recently if I remembered that in the beginning, he had wanted to give Joe some seed money to gamble with. I don't remember any mention of that, probably because it made my head twist around in circles while smoke came out of my ears. I considered gambling to be an example of what people who lacked motivation and direction did when they weren't standing in the street with a sign that said, "Will work for food." That is the nicest way I can say that; what I thought was much worse.

Now I wonder about all the people who quit work to play poker during the poker boom. What happened to all those accountants, teachers, lawyers, students, and parents of young children who gave up job security to play cards competitively? I suppose they ruined their finances and had to start over.

Why couldn't I have accepted my son's choice with grace and compassion? Then he might have gotten sick of it like the rest of the world, and he might be here today, laughing about his foolish youth as a riverboat gambler.

Once when Jim, Joe, and I were in the supermarket together, a young man came up to Joe and asked, "Hey, how are you doing?" I could see they knew each other, and the next time Jim and I saw the man, we greeted him.

"Are you Joe's parents?" he asked.

"Yes, how do you know him?"

"He works here at night with me, stocking shelves."

Another thing we hadn't known and didn't understand.

Our son's all-consuming interest in poker seemed as risky as standing on a log heading for a waterfall. One night when the fog was so thick there was almost no visibility, I drove him to the casino. On the entrance ramp, a derelict suddenly stepped out of the mist and almost walked into our car. As I yanked the steering wheel and swerved to avoid hitting the bum, I sputtered, "What was *that*?"

"Desperation," Joe answered.

It occurred to me that he chose that word because he knew the feeling and he was headed in the same direction. No doubt there is a career to be made in every kind of weird thing. If your passion in life is solving crossword puzzles, you can create them, publish books of them, and sell copies of puzzles to newspapers. I have an open mind about following your passion on the road less traveled, and I wanted to support my son's choices . . . but his decision to play cards as a job was simply beyond my comprehension.

There was so much we did not know about Joe that, as time passed, I felt less sure that anything we did was useful. All I do know is that I didn't believe he was living the life he really wanted to live, and I thought he needed to be fixed. Now, when I look at pictures of him carrying his nephews on his shoulders to the ice cream store, I see the sadness in his face, and the empty look in his eyes breaks my heart.

Whether he'd experienced a financial failure, a bad breakup, a major depressive breakdown—or all three—I'll never know. But in retrospect, I know he needed help and healing. At the time, I couldn't identify what my eyes saw, and I didn't know what to do about it.

11 The Elephant in the Room

For long periods of time, we didn't see Joe, and when we did see him, I refused to acknowledge he could be as lost as he looked. I tried to convince myself everything was going to be okay. And yet one evening when we were all together at the Shore, Joe suddenly appeared in the dark doorway near our dining room. He had been working (i.e., playing poker) in Atlantic City. He was unsmiling, unshaven, and wearing a dark sweatshirt and old Villanova baseball cap. He looked like those card players you see on the TV poker shows. When I introduced him to his cousins, I heard one of their parents ask the other, "Who does he look like?" (meaning "does he look like his mom or his dad?"), and the answer I heard was "mental illness."

I pretended I didn't hear.

I've thought about this a lot, and I still don't know what I should or could have done. The way Joe looked during the years he was gambling and the situation he seemed to be in were unthinkable. I only know what I should *not* have done. I should not have allowed the elephant to live with us. So many of us grow up with an elephant in the room, and marry someone who also grew up with an elephant in their room, that we're so used to it we don't react to the hoofprints in our own home. The zoo has become normalized.

After our awkward start at the Shore in 2005, we tried to be friends. Joe showed us spreadsheets that tracked hours at the card tables, his return on investment, and the likelihood of winning with two decks versus one. He kept meticulous records of all sorts of folderol I never understood or cared to understand. He even introduced us to one of his new friends, a man as somber as a mortician who had retired from a successful career and now used his pension to gamble full time. He and Joe talked about their experiences at the tables, on the river, and through the flops; they even compared spreadsheets.

The man and his family were apparently happy with his gambling career; it was something he could afford to do. I compared the man's situation to my son's. Joe didn't have a wife or family to support, nor did he have money, transportation, insurance, or a job. He owned nothing of value, and he didn't have a plan. There was no comparison, no security, and no career for Joe in that scenario.

I couldn't accept it, and part of the time I went bananas. I don't want to say that Jim and I almost got divorced over it, but I couldn't stand the fact that sometimes Jim would go gambling with Joe, and they would talk about the river and the flop as though they had just had a great afternoon on the golf course. It was totally unacceptable to me—in fact it seemed like encouraging a diabetic to get a job as a candy taster. Sometimes I wasn't sure who the diabetic was.

I was a mess by proxy. By that, I mean I blamed Joe for my issues, as though his behavior were the cause of everything wrong in my life. Today, I am stunned by the extent of my efforts to change him into what I wanted him to be.

Joe was stoic, disdainful of my quick tears, and annoyed by my never-ending desire to motivate and fix him. I just could not think of gambling as a profession because the outcome of a game of chance is not predictable. A paycheck is predictable. In my ignorance, I prattled on about things other people's children did . . . the things I wished he would do—like get a job in the industry he was trained for, or make a different choice, or go back to school and become a history professor. The only thing I knew for sure was that his mind was too good to be wasted.

My son once told me that gambling was his dream job, and that there were many people in the gaming industry who had successful careers and shared his opinion. I told him that day that I felt bad for being so unsupportive in the past. In the future, I said, I would be more understanding. I meant every word when I said it.

But as time passed, my son's life, which was not mine to control, became my main focus. I used it as an excuse for my anger, my disappointment, and my general unhappiness. I let his behavior control me. Looking back, I recognize this now as codependence.

There is an old book called *Codependent No More*, by Melody Beattie, that I had to read for one of my psychology classes. It was there on my bookshelf, but I doubt it could have helped me when I needed it; I was too obtuse to recognize myself.

Nonetheless, quietly and secretly, while paying rent to us and living in the attic apartment, Joe became a casino slots attendant. I didn't realize how much work getting this job required of my son until I saw his personal papers after his death. In order to pass a background check and have a good credit report, he had to hire a lawyer and file two years of back tax returns, with interest and penalties, in preparation for his petition to the gaming commission for permission to work in a casino.

If I am right and he was clinically depressed, it must have been nearly impossible for him to pull himself together to get organized and out of his situation without help or handout, but he did it. I guess he stocked shelves in that supermarket for a good reason. His remarkable recovery is not only noteworthy, it was another big secret.

Soon he was managing slots, and when it seemed like he was on his feet, we told him we were going to sell the Shore house because I was on the list for a heart transplant, and we needed to simplify our lives. We explained it would probably be a year before we put the house on the market, because we wanted him to have plenty of time to make new arrangements for himself.

He surprised us by renting an apartment in Brigantine, New Jersey, and buying a car and new furniture. He was well-dressed again, and he invited us over to see his new place. It was wonderful. He worked on a casino sales team with *whales*, customers who regularly gamble large amounts and are rewarded by the casinos with hotel rooms, fancy restaurant meals, trips, and cruises—all designed to make them loyal losers, because ultimately everyone loses.

At one point I criticized this job choice. "I don't get it," I said. "You know they are going to lose money; that's the business model. No matter what they do, the casino will make money. How can you encourage gambling behavior to people who probably already overdo it?"

Joe just shrugged. "Well, they like the service."

"But how do you feel about doing it?"

"I understand them," he said. "We have the same disease."

It was the only time I ever heard him admit that gambling might have been a negative factor in his life.

Gambling is part of our family culture. Jim's father was a prodigious horse-racing enthusiast and publisher of the *Daily Racing Form*. When Jim and I were newly married and living in San Diego, his dad visited and took us to the races at Del Mar. We had grand seats, and Mr. Hooker seemed to know everyone who worked at the track and with the horses. By the time he had received a gazillion unsolicited tips and placed all his bets, he had a fistful of tickets. At the end of the last race, as we were walking out, he threw all his tickets away before he remembered that one was a winner. I said, "Let's go back to our seats. I know where that ticket is." But he said it wasn't worth the bother. I couldn't imagine doing such a thing.

One of the things Jim received after his father died was a gambling diary from 1973. The notebook began on January 1, with a statement in his dad's handwriting that explained that he was keeping a record of his wagers to satisfy his wife's curiosity about how much money he was spending at the racetrack. There were tickets from various racetracks stapled to pages several times a week for five months. Then the record stops and the results are tallied; the losses totaled $29,971 and change. I wondered how much money that would be in 2023 dollars, so I asked Google, and found that $29,971 in 1973 would be worth $212,899.58 in 2023. Amazing!

Growing up in a competitive family of three boys and one girl, Jim, his siblings, and their parents were bridge players, ball players, golfers, and poker players. Jim used to love games of chance, and he invented silly games to play with our children. He continues them now with our grandkids—games like How Much Money's in My Pocket? That game started with jingling coins when they were little, but as they have grown older, the game has changed to a wad of one-dollar bills with a higher denomination hidden in the middle. Everyone sees the fistful of dollars and each guesses an amount; the closest one wins the pot. It is pretty exciting when we are all together for a holiday, and Jim holds a wad of money over his head and a circle of little and not-so-little people jump around him shouting numbers.

Our family also bets on March Madness and the Kentucky Derby. Not large amounts of money, but enough to liven up an impromptu gathering. Jim picks up card games easily and knows how to play all kinds. It is a lot of fun, although strange to me. In my family, money was a serious subject; there were no random bets. Consequently, I have never understood how gambling is of any interest to anyone. Some people enjoy games and some make careers of them. But I have zero interest in that kind of competition; I don't understand its purpose nor the satisfaction anyone receives from it.

My benign disinterest changed as I watched Joe's downward spiral. I became increasingly negative about gambling's effect on his life and health. At a casino, people gamble, drink, and smoke all night long. The hangover can be more painful than a migraine, especially if the gambler was too impaired to make sound decisions and risked money he didn't have, to recover money he had already lost. I do not think gambling is inherently wrong, but I think Joe had a weakness for it. Watching him suffer from the consequences of losing made my aversion increasingly strong.

Joe always said he could not gamble while he worked for a casino; it was a rule in the industry. Unfortunately, most of the time he did not work for a casino.

The most surprising thing was, after he died and we met his friends, not even one of them thought he gambled. I don't know how to explain it. Either he was a professional gambler and gambled right up until his death but never told his friends, or he hid his addiction to gambling. Or maybe he never was addicted, but he was so angry with my constant presumption, that he would not dignify it with a response. He certainly didn't think he owed us an explanation for anything else.

12 THE MOVE TO LAS VEGAS

When Atlantic City suffered a major downturn in 2008, Joe was one of two workers on his team who were offered positions in Las Vegas. His relocation package provided a room in the Hard Rock Hotel. The real estate market in Las Vegas was in a freefall, and after growing up in a family that recognized the value of investing in residential real estate, he was ready to buy. I had helped his sisters buy houses, and I wanted to help him too.

When he said, "This might be the greatest real estate market of my lifetime, and I should buy a house," I was jubilant. My hope for Joe was simple: he would buy a house, get a dog, fall in love, get married, have 2.6 children, and make me happy. A house has a way of grounding people, and I assumed he would get a great deal of pleasure from owning and improving his own home. I suggested that he get his real estate license and work in the industry in his spare time as a way to find a good deal for himself. With the overabundance of inventory, scarcity of buyers, and a growing number of flippers, there had to be countless opportunities.

But Joe wasn't interested in a real estate license. He had a full-time casino job and wanted to enjoy his time off, so I contacted a real estate agent who knew of a great house. Joe signed a contract as soon as he saw it. He was supposed to leave a check but decided not to since he didn't like the closing costs, didn't like the idea of his check being cashed and held in escrow before settlement, and didn't like the fact that owners and banks would not consider contracts contingent on home inspections.

The agent wanted him to go to a settlement with very little information. It seemed to be a good deal at the time, but the speed with which it happened made him uneasy. The fact that there was an excessive number of available houses, people who squatted in houses that they didn't own, and prices that continued to plummet made Joe suspect that all the information he'd received was tainted.

He described the market as broken, and he was correct. Houses were being sold "as is" for half their initial purchase price, and some owners left their keys on the counter and drove away. Investors scooped up foreclosed properties and managed them as rentals. It was chaotic.

Meanwhile, Joe was worried that he would own a house before he knew whether it had problems. I told him that, of course there would be problems, maybe even disasters, because the best deals are abandoned houses in poor condition. The reason for a fire sale is the fire; a deplorable condition is the reason for a price that's too good to pass up. Banks that sold foreclosures "as is" were taking a huge loss because they wanted to be done with the property immediately, before a buyer had an inspection, or expected repairs or got cold feet.

For a while, he called me with addresses, and I'd look them up and we'd talk about the process and the prices. He even thought about buying a condo because it was cheaper than renting a room. But I didn't encourage that idea. There were so many empty and abandoned condos it was almost impossible to have confidence in their future investment value. Many homeowner associations were financially under water. It was not unusual to drive into a condo development and find dead birds in a half-empty swimming pool.

Joe saw houses with several agents before he decided that buying a trashed house and fixing it up was more trouble than it was worth. Besides, no property ever seemed as good as the house he'd walked away from on the first day. Before long, his relocation package was gone, and his free room at the Hard Rock Hotel was no longer free.

Looking to save what was left of his potential downpayment money while he shopped for a house, he decided against finding an apartment, and opted for a room he found on Craigslist instead. Everything was fine until the day he came home from work to find an eviction notice on the front door. His landlord sat inside watching TV.

"What's up with the eviction notice?" Joe asked.

"This isn't my house," the man said. "I was paying rent to somebody who didn't own the place. Now we both have to get out."

Joe started anew, looking for possibilities on Craigslist. The next one he chose was in a house with a woman and her teenage son. Her husband had moved in with his girlfriend and left his wife unable to pay the mortgage, so she was renting out a room. Unfortunately, when the husband found out his wife had rented a room to a man, he rushed back and changed the locks.

Joe arrived home to find that his key no longer worked. No one answered the door, but through a back window he could see what he was convinced was the three months' rent he'd had to pay in advance to move in. He called to tell me he wanted to break the window and take his money back.

"No, don't do that," I said. "You don't want to deal with the repercussions if you get caught breaking into that house, even to take your own money. You do that, and we have a real problem. It's awful that they've done this to you, and it's worse that they're going to get away with it, but the woman is probably in a very bad place and needs money more than you do. You can recover; I'll send you money for another place, and you can go on with life. Just walk away and forget about it. You are not so desperate that you would risk jail."

I put money in his account, Joe found another room, and I heard no more about it. Before long, a coworker at the casino introduced Joe to her unemployed husband who was attempting to start a call center. The two men shared an interest in being their own boss. Joe was familiar with call centers; he had surprised us by working at one while he was in high school. We knew from our own experience that he had an innate talent for talking people into buying things they didn't want to buy and doing things they didn't want to do.

Joe and his new friend developed a pitch for a group of angel investors and received a $50,000 loan to launch their new business. Joe walked away from his hard-won book of clients, quit the job that had brought him to Las Vegas, and went all-in on the call center. He and his partner found inexpensive office space in a good location because it had belonged to another undercapitalized business that had failed.

The office was near a bus stop, a big plus because they expected to hire employees who needed public transportation. Despite their lack of experience, they negotiated a commercial lease, and as soon as it was signed, they became anxious to earn the funds to pay back the money they had borrowed, the money they were spending, and the money they needed to provide payroll for the people they expected to hire. It was intense, and I noticed that neither of them mentioned when they might be able to pay themselves.

At an unpaid storage auction, they bought a garage full of abandoned office furniture. We received pictures of an empty office with piles of gray-fabric cubby walls, metal forms, partitions, and assorted parts of desks, shelves, and chairs. Despite a lack of instructions, proper tools, and a shortage of connection pieces, Joe spent at least a week building desks and workstations between naps on the office floor.

It was a marvel to us that he'd built an office from scratch. He must have been born with that knowledge because he had not learned any practical skills in our home.

A few months into this venture, our daughter, Jennifer, moved to a new job in San Francisco. I drove cross-country with her, and we stopped in Las Vegas to see Joe. He showed us around, and we were amazed when we saw the terrific office they were creating.

To save the cost of newspaper advertising, Joe had visited the unemployment office in person to get employees. On one side of the office space, he constructed workstations, and on the other side, his partner interviewed potential workers. They both trained, made calls, and solicited potential clients. It was a three-ring circus of activity, and I was proud of my son.

The call center was doing remarkably well, but when it was time for their first client to pay his bill, he delayed, made excuses, and finally said he wasn't satisfied with the number of calls or the results. His refusal to pay meant that there were no funds for the first payroll, and the staff simply walked out.

A letter from a lawyer threatening to enforce the contract might have been enough to scare the client into compliance, but it takes money to hire a lawyer and the start-up money was gone. There was no money to pay rent and utilities and none to repay the angel fund. Joe had given up his apartment and was sleeping on his friend's couch. His old job was gone, his attempt to start the call center had collapsed, and his partner/friend packed up his family and moved to a faraway state.

It was the beginning of the end.

Still, Joe didn't tell us what was happening, and he didn't answer questions about it, either. What I remember, as I sit here three years after his death, is that he drove home for Christmas and had virtually nothing with him. He insisted on putting his car in our garage and didn't drive it until the day he left; he would not drive one of our cars, and every time he wanted to go to the store, he expected one of us to drive him and pay. We soon noticed that his car registration had expired, but we didn't mention it . . . and neither did he. No one said a word, but we all knew, and he knew that we knew.

He gave no Christmas gifts that year, not even a card. We did not call him on his behavior because we were used to it, and we wanted a peaceful holiday. It never occurred to me that he was actually broke; I just thought he was cheap. I couldn't believe our smart, terrific son could look so lost. It was inconceivable. I was annoyed that he had come home without decent clothes, unprepared to even go to a relative's home for a holiday party.

He put his clothes in the washer and when I moved them to the dryer, I couldn't help but notice that they were no better than rags.

Without saying a word, I threw some of them into the garbage, then went to the store and replaced them. Furious, I let myself imagine that he was purposely trying to get our sympathy so that we would give him more money. I took him to a men's store and bought him three nice casual outfits. The way he touched the fabric on one of the shirts showed me how much he liked the idea of wearing something that would look great on him. But he went quietly up to his room with the bags, and the next day he told me he didn't want the clothes because he had no place to wear them. He asked me to take them back, and I did.

We expected him to take off when he felt like it, without telling us. And I am sure every one of us asked him when he was going back to Las Vegas; my intention was to make sure I had some cash to give him and to be around to see him off when he decided to go. We wanted to wish him well. But he mostly stayed in his room. When we did see him, he was fussy.

One day, he snapped at me. "Don't ask me when I'm leaving again!" he said. "I'm not going to tell you when I'm leaving!"

I realize now that our curiosity was probably annoying. I wonder if he might have wanted to stay with us, but our constant asking about his departure made him feel unwanted. If I'd have known, I'd have asked him to stay, but it didn't occur to me. He acted like he didn't want to be around us.

We didn't pay attention to his circumstances because we couldn't see them. It wasn't possible that it could be as bad as it looked. I still can't believe what it might have been. But he studiously avoided all discussion of himself and his plans.

On the day he left, I gave him $600 for the trip, but at the last minute, as he stood in the doorway of his room (up earlier than he wanted to be because the cleaning lady was at our house making a lot of noise), he looked at me and said very quietly, "But I have nowhere to go."

Putting these events in order for the first time, I now realize he might really have had no place to go. At the time, I thought nothing of it. If you had asked me, I might have guessed he meant he hadn't decided whether he was taking the southern or northern route. Now, however, I hear those quiet, offhand words as loud as a locomotive, and I wonder if his partner/friend's couch had been Joe's home until the friend and his family moved far away, and Joe was going back after Christmas to face the music alone.

Later he called me and spoke about the investors wanting to be paid back. I told him there was nothing he could do; the business had failed. It was like *Shark Tank*. I said, "Sometimes people invest in businesses that fail."

"But people worked, Mom. They deserve to be paid. It's the right thing to do."

I sighed. "How much would it take to make payroll?"

"Twenty-five thousand dollars," he answered.

"I could take that out of my IRA," I answered. "Do you want me to?"

"No," he responded. "I wouldn't."

So I didn't, and we never spoke of it again. He called me to say that a friend had let him stay in her home while she went on vacation, but he hadn't realized the bathroom was under construction, the utilities had been turned off, and there was no air conditioning. He called a few times after that and asked me to transfer enough money for a night in a hotel so he could sleep, and I did.

13 Fibromyalgia, the Mystery Disease

In 2014, Joe called and asked me to transfer money into his account so he could buy some work clothes; he had just been hired by Ford and he was happy about it. Considering his past experience in the car business, he could easily have been the finance manager of the dealership, but at Ford, all new employees begin in the car lot. He loved the idea that everyone starts at the bottom, selling cars. Despite the Las Vegas heat, Joe enjoyed selling cars. He was really good at playing with the numbers until a deal was irresistible, and people loved him. One week he called to tell me he'd sold ten cars, but he didn't feel well.

Even as a child with allergies and asthma-induced breathing problems, he'd never complained about how he felt—he'd just retreated to his room with a book and waited it out. But when unrelenting pain in his ribs made it almost impossible to get in and out of a car, he went to his supervisor and said, "I think I have a broken rib, and I'd like to work at an inside job temporarily until a doctor figures out what's wrong."

He could've done a hundred other jobs, but his supervisor wouldn't go for it. After a month of undiagnosed pain and after being terminated because he couldn't get in and out of a car, a doctor told Joe he had fibromyalgia, a medical disorder with symptoms of musculoskeletal pain and fatigue, a condition so vague it is sometimes faked.

I couldn't imagine how bad the pain in his side must have been for him to actually go to a doctor. He called me, fuming. "Fibromyalgia is a bulls**t diagnosis! This pain is not something I am making up."

Jim and I were worried. We went to Las Vegas for the Thanksgiving weekend in 2014 to see for ourselves. Joe's still unregistered car needed new tires and multiple repairs before it could pass inspection. It took his father two days in lines at the DMV to pay his fines and penalties. It cost thousands before the car was legal to drive.

Joe was still convinced he had a broken rib. After Thanksgiving, Jim flew home, but I couldn't leave. I stayed despite the fact that there was nothing I could do, and Joe said he didn't want me there. I told him I could not leave him alone and sick, and I moved from our hotel to a small apartment near him and rented a TV and a few pieces of furniture. I did what I wanted after my heart transplant because I felt the pressure of life on borrowed time. Jim didn't argue with me because he didn't know how to stop this new brave me. And Joe picked me up for lunch every few days because I didn't have a car.

It wasn't long before Joe started another new job, and Jim drove to Las Vegas to bring our dog to me. Joe still had no real diagnosis, but new X-rays showed that a number of tumors had broken through his ribs. When he asked if I wanted to go to the doctor with him, I silently rejoiced.

His taciturn lady doctor had neither a smile nor a funny bone in her body, but I could tell he liked her. At one point there was a pause in their seemingly unproductive conversation, and I jumped in. "What do you *think* is wrong with him, Doctor? You must have an idea."

She paused, then replied in her heavy Russian accent, "It could be multiple myeloma."

"What?" I was unable to breathe.

"Multiple myeloma," she repeated. "A urinalysis could confirm it."

"Like right now, a urinalysis would tell you?"

She nodded and turned to Joe. "Do you want to take a test right now?"

"Yes!" he said.

"I'll be right back."

Fifteen minutes later she came back and said, "I have to see another patient now. Take this prescription to the lab and tell them it is the test for multiple myeloma."

The room felt crowded, as though the space was shrinking.

Joe took the prescription, but when we got to the laboratory, they would not do the test because the doctor had written it on the wrong prescription pad. We decided to take a break from doctors and go to the Bagel Café. We'd had enough for that day.

When Joe was finally diagnosed with multiple myeloma (MM), Jim called his nephew, Dr. Thomas Hooker, a respected Pulmonologist and fellow Villanova alum. Dr. Tom spoke to the Russian doctor and reviewed Joe's X-rays. Then he explained the bad news to Joe, and later, to us in language we all understood. He told us there were lesions in Joe's ribs, chest, shoulder, arm, and leg. Soft-tissue tumors associated with bone lesions are indicative of the worst MM outcomes, but no one told us that, and I didn't have the courage to look it up until I wrote this chapter in 2022.

In MM, cancerous plasma cells escape through bone lesions and cause tumors; one on his clavicle was the size of a golf ball and quite visible. Each plasma cell can produce thousands of antibodies in seconds, to save our life with an immune response during a health crisis. Cancer (abnormal cells) can clone unnoticed for ten years before the marrow is so full that soft tumors break through bones that have been destroyed from the inside. The pain is terrible, and that is how MM is usually discovered.

Dr. Tom urged us to start radiation therapy immediately to reduce the size of his tumors. After a couple days of negotiation, the Russian lady doctor decided to admit him to the hospital through the emergency room, just before Christmas. When we took him to the downtown Las Vegas emergency room, the ER doctor asked, "Why are you here?"

Joe said he was there to start treatment for multiple myeloma, and the ER doctor said, "That's not an emergency."

We were shocked that as desperate as we were to have him begin treatment, the doctors did not seem to think time was of the essence. If it hadn't been for the help we had, I can't imagine how long it would have been before there was any forward motion in his situation. Anyway, despite the nonemergency, they kept Joe in the hospital, and treatment began. The doctor who admitted him that day was the doctor who took care of him in the hospital, after his eventual stem cell transplant, and, in fact, for the whole time he was in Las Vegas.

Jennifer flew out to spend the holiday with us, although we had no celebration at all. I bought a miniature tree, and we wrote Christmas wishes for each other and put them in a jar. I think I was in charge of that, and it was pretty lame. To me, it didn't seem as much like Christmas as it did the end of the world.

Joe was alive, but like anyone who has an incurable disease, he was already dying; multiple myeloma doesn't allow its victims to ignore the fact that their time is limited. Pain, impending fractures, exhaustion, and lack of hope take the joy out of most days, while treatments and maintenance therapy make it impossible to forget the brevity of life.

When Joe was diagnosed, life expectancy was two years. There is still no cure. Even after a successful stem cell transplant when they find no MM cells in a blood test, the disease remains, and it will return.

After Joe's transplant, they did not remove the chemo port in his neck because it was necessary to check his blood every three months for a "bloom" (abnormal cells that indicate the disease is back). And he had to continue to receive Revlimid, a maintenance chemo.

There are endless opportunities for anxiety and despair when recurrence is a certainty. Hope lies in the discovery of new drugs that will change MM from fatal to chronic. In the meantime, patients take pain meds and a plethora of drugs with lethal side effects.

Despite Joe's diagnosis, pain, uncertain job prospects, financial failures, and gambling problems, he seldom complained. Still, his situation created a perfect storm of hopelessness, and I can only wonder how he managed to carry that load by himself for as long as he did.

14 A Party to Remember

Las Vegas seems like a place of great wealth where you would expect to find the cutting edge of medical innovation, but it did not have a hospital that performed transplants. Joe's doctor sent him to the University of Arizona Cancer Center in Tucson, for an autologous stem cell transplant (using his own cells) in May of 2015. The prospect of Joe receiving the best treatment available gave me the confidence to move out of my apartment and drive home to North Carolina with Jim.

Joe told his friends at the Gin Mill, a neighborhood bar near his apartment, about the stem cell transplant, a treatment he was not confident he would survive. They asked if there was anything they could do, and he suggested a party—one they could all remember.

After his death, we were surprised to hear about that party from his friends. It makes me sad that he didn't mention it when he was alive, and we weren't invited. It makes me even more sad to know that our presence probably would have ruined it for him. But one thing is certain, it sounds exactly like what Joe would do, and we are glad he had a great party.

The idea was an instant hit; the Gin Mill staff threw themselves into preparations.

After sampling a wide range of concoctions to create a signature drink for the event, Joe selected his favorite, an exotic purple brew they named the "Little Joe." Its ingredients included curaçao, purple cherry vodka, Red Bull, grenadine, and a secret sauce. They had seventy-five *Little Joe* labels made for the small mugs and poured the crazy purple mixture into them on the night of the event. When the

Little Joe shots were served, Joe raised his mug and toasted, "Here's to us and those like us. Damn few left!"

The crowd raised their mugs and drank. "Hear! Hear!"

Joe loved poems and movies. At the appropriate point in a conversation with his inner circle, he would start a quote from a film and one of them would finish it. *Shawshank Redemption* was one of his favorites.

He would say, "Whether you think you can, or you think you can't—"

And someone would answer, "You're right."

Or he'd say, "You'd better get busy living—"

And someone would reply, "Or get busy dying."

It was very cool. It was also very Joe—sometimes he would start a phone call with, "This is Carlton, your doorman," from the *Rhoda* TV show.

I remember asking him to explain a comment he'd made once, and he replied, "I'm like the man who carried such a large bundle of sticks that the only way to pick up a new one was to put an old one down." At the time I thought he was quoting from a movie or one of his favorite books, but now I think he was telling me he was at his limit.

Three years later, when Joe's friends didn't see him at the Gin Mill on New Year's Eve, they inquired, and when word spread about his death, they decided he would like another party, just like the original one in 2015 before his stem cell transplant. They knew what he liked—he had helped plan the first party and most of the decorations were still at the bar.

The waitresses had their favorite picture of him printed on black T-shirts for the celebration of Joe's life after his death. Under his likeness were the words, "Forever in our hearts, Big Joe." They made the purple potion to serve in the little mugs, and the mood was beyond nostalgic.

His friends told me about both parties—the one before his stem cell transplant, and with greater excitement, the one three years later after his death.

Joe's friends Steve, Jacquie, and Matt were sitting at the horseshoe-shaped bar, and Matt was playing one of the video poker machines. Suddenly, he felt Joe's presence. Looking up, he said, "Joe, if you're here, send us a sign." When he pulled the handle of the machine, lights flashed and bells began to ring. The machine hit a Royal Flush, and everyone clapped and hooted.

Matt, Steve, and Jacquie looked at each other, then shouted, "He's here! Joe's here!"

The noise and lights continued as a second and then a third machine also hit a Royal Flush. It was amazing and magical. His friends were fully convinced of his presence.

"Joe is here!" they shouted, and raised their glasses to toast him, while Billy Joel sang.

As I wrote this, I realized someone might have made up the part about the Royal Flushes just to make me feel good. I wondered about the mathematical probability of three royal flushes, and I knew that if I told this story to Joe, he would have laughed and said, "My BS meter is going off." So I decided to check.

On October 21, 2020, at 2:30 P.M. EST, I called the Gin Mill. Someone answered the phone and I asked for Stephanie, the only name I remembered.

"She's off today. I'm Jena. Can I help you?"

I asked if the Gin Mill was a casino, and she said, "Not technically. We don't have any slot machines. But there are fifteen video poker machines around a horseshoe bar."

I explained that I was Joe Hooker's mom and that I had heard a story about three of the poker machines hitting jackpots during the party after his death. Jena told me she had worked that night, and the story was definitely true. She said they still had Joe's picture on display at the bar, and she was looking at him as we spoke. She said his name still comes up; he is remembered and missed.

I was a mess by then, but pulled myself together and texted Joe's friend Matt to ask him about the Royal Flush jackpots. He, too, said it was true; he was one of the three people whose machine had hit one. I am still amazed.

I wanted to see the Gin Mill, so when Jennifer went to Las Vegas for a work conference in 2019, I flew there and we went together. It was small and dark. Its ancient jukebox was stocked with U2, Bruce Springsteen, and all Joe's favorites. I learned that sometimes, when a Billy Joel song was playing, Joe would grab a karaoke mike and sing along. I would not have believed that, but they gave me a video to prove it.

While we were there, Jen and I saw his usual parking spot out front and sat at his favorite spot at the bar. We even drank a Little Joe shot. His friends were there, and everyone who came into the bar passed by our chairs and said hi. It was reminiscent of the *Cheers* TV show, but sad.

15 Stem Cell Transplant

Joe's stem cell transplant was scheduled for May 2015, in Tucson. He was required to bring a caretaker who was free to relocate for several months. Jennifer wanted to help him, and she flew out to meet with the doctors. However, she had just relocated to San Francisco and her employer refused to give her the time off to help Joe. After his treatment, she would have been without a job or a place to live. She and Joe were disappointed, and so were we.

I had insisted that I wanted to be there from the first mention of a stem cell transplant, but in my heart of hearts, I didn't think I was up to the task. I was seventy-three years old with a transplanted heart. Jim was absolutely against my going. He was sure it would kill me, and he insisted that if I went, he was coming to take care of me.

Joe was dead set against Jim being there. Even as a child, Joe hadn't wanted people around when he didn't feel well, and with all his asthma and allergy attacks, I think he'd already had his fill of doctors. Joe had always preferred to remain quiet in his room with a book while he recovered, and we understood that he did not want company. This was no different. Joe was Joe, and we would have felt the same way about having our kids take care of us.

"Dad can't come," Joe insisted. "Don't do this to me." But Joe had no idea what it was like to live with us now. He didn't know the physical limitations the heart transplant had imposed upon me, and he saw me as far more capable than I was.

When I hung up the phone, Jim said, "I'm going anyway."

I was used to Jim's overpowering help, and to tell the truth, I liked it. I couldn't take care of anyone but myself at that point, and it took two of us to do that. Since my heart transplant in 2011, Jim had been jumping up to do things I should have done alone. I allowed him to be overprotective because it was easier to be babied than to step up and take over. As a result, I *talked about* independence, but I *lived in* dependence. If Jim's efforts were controlling, I realized that was how he handled his fear that I would push myself too far, too fast.

Besides, Jim always has endless energy and a positive attitude. I knew I couldn't take care of Joe alone, and I didn't know what else to do. So, as usual, I did nothing. The day we were supposed to check in at Tucson rumbled toward us like a huge storm cloud that could unleash enough rain to cause a tsunami in the Arizona desert.

I realize now that I didn't need to be capable of taking care of anyone by myself; there are professional healthcare workers to take care of the patient. I just needed to sit by Joe's bed and be present in case he needed someone to advocate for him or to listen or just to *be there* for him. That's what I wish I had done. As it turned out, Jim and I were both there, but neither of us were present. We didn't sit around and have deep conversations with Joe; he wasn't interested. In fact, he was angry we were there. He told us—after the fact—that his insurance would have paid for a professional caretaker.

I doubt it would have mattered to me, anyway. I ignored his wishes when I insisted on being there, and then I wallowed in self-pity because I was not wanted. We floundered around like three strangers in a lifeboat.

The day arrived as if it were a normal day. Jim and I traveled from Fairfax, Virginia, to Tucson. Joe had already driven down from Las Vegas and checked into the hospital for two days of stem cell harvest. We settled into the apartment prepared for us on hospital grounds, while Joe underwent the stem cell retrieval in the operating room.

Stem cells in our bone marrow are with us from birth; their supply is limited and cannot be reproduced. They are able to go anywhere in the body and adapt to do the job required; they can repair injury and cure cancer. The most beautiful thing about them is that they cannot be rejected by the body that made them. Using donated stem cells would have run that risk.

The harvesting of Joe's stem cells took place under general anesthesia so he wouldn't feel the pain of the special needle that aspirated a liter of bone marrow from several places on his hip bone. Afterward, a deafening plasmapheresis machine separated the damaged and cancerous cells from the marrow while Joe was treated with a very high dose of chemo in a process called "conditioning," which destroys any remaining cancer cells in the body.

At the same time, his immune system was suppressed to reduce the chance that his body would reject the transplanted cells, and a central line was inserted into a large vein near his heart so that he could receive the stem cells and medication instantly. The conditioning process, and the actual transplant—the process of returning the stem cells to his body—took place while Joe was an inpatient.

Joe ordinarily avoided doctors at all costs. I cannot imagine how traumatic this procedure was for him. The conscious mind does not remember the pain and sounds of unpleasant medical procedures, but even when we are unconscious, traumatic events like this cause adrenaline and other neurochemicals to rush to the site and record the memory.

Joe's doctor successfully harvested enough cells for two transplants: one batch for immediate use, and the other to be cryopreserved for a later time as needed. The cells were stored at the cancer center.

When Joe had no detectable immune system remaining, he received the conditioning chemo designed to kill all the cancer cells left. We watched him through a window, delirious for days, with a temperature hovering around 105 degrees. Every morning, the medical staff posted the results of his blood tests on the whiteboard in his room. Finally, the day came when they warmed his stem cells in his circulating blood and returned them to his body. Then we waited, eager for the cells to find their way to his bone marrow and to multiply and reestablish his immune system.

Meanwhile, we made an appointment to speak to someone about his treatment; we'd been paying his co-pays forever, but we could see literature everywhere that advised patients to apply for price breaks from pharmaceutical companies. At our appointment, we were told Joe had not signed the paperwork that would allow us to speak to his doctors, so we couldn't go to any of his appointments.

We asked if they would mention the possibility of getting a break on his co-pay charges to him so that he could apply; but we were told he made too much money to get the discount. That was a surprise to us, but... we did not speak to him about it.

Joe had lost what was left of his hair, and according to the whiteboard that tracked his vitals, he had also lost fifty pounds. I was terrified that his brain would be damaged by his high temperatures. Only the nurses could enter his room, but the first thing we did every morning was look through his window at the chart on the wall, to see if any antibodies had been found in his blood. The number started at zero; and just when we were on our last nerve and had decided that the treatment was worse than the disease, a few cells were counted. A nurse erased the zero and told us Joe's immune system had rebooted.

A group of nurses came to sing "Happy Birthday," and told Joe he was born again like a baby with no protection against childhood diseases, the common cold, or even the simplest germs. They said he would receive baby shots when he was stronger, and before long he was allowed to come back to our apartment on the hospital grounds.

Joe had health insurance from his employer that covered his treatment and his caregiver expenses (if he'd keep a record and file a claim), but he didn't keep records. Jim put all his receipts in a paper bag and later filed the claim for Joe. When the reimbursement check arrived, Joe sent it to us, and we sent it back to him.

Because he was vulnerable to common germs, his apartment in Las Vegas needed to be deep-cleaned before he could return to it. He mentioned that one night at 10:00 P.M., just as we were heading to bed, and said he didn't know how he was going to get it done. We suggested calling the property-management office in the morning to hire someone. He didn't respond. Instead, he told us he was going to drive to Las Vegas to "take care of some things." He said he'd be back in time for his doctor's appointment at ten the next morning and left the room.

It took a minute for us to absorb the news that he was leaving the hospital grounds, which was not allowed, driving the car, which was not allowed, and going to Las Vegas, which was hours away. Jim didn't want me to report him AWOL because he was afraid Joe would be dismissed from treatment, but I was afraid he would die, literally.

While Jim and I argued about what to do, Joe left in his car.

Finally, Jim caved. "Go ahead and call," he said. And I called the doctor's emergency number. I asked the doctor on duty to call Joe and talk him into coming back. I said I was afraid he would die. We were so worried about his safety, we expected a big explosion. But after we reported the emergency, no one called us back. We finally went to bed, and Joe was not in the apartment when we woke the next morning.

Since he wasn't supposed to drive, I had been driving him back and forth to his appointments in our car. This time I went alone and sat in the waiting room, wondering what would happen next. Joe arrived at the last minute, and since I was not allowed in the room with the doctor, I have no idea if there was any discussion of his escape. When we silently walked out to my rental car, it was parked next to a new Ford hybrid. Standing beside me, Joe said, "I traded in my car."

I was so dumbfounded that I didn't ask if he had also arranged to have his apartment cleaned. Privately, I sputtered to Jim about all the time and money he had spent getting his car drivable, but he just said the repairs had probably made it a good trade-in. There was no way to predict what Joe would do.

We had watched his delirious suffering for days and had prayed while he was attached to the deafening plasmapheresis machine. His treatment was now over, and he was considered in remission, but he was as weak as a baby and still sick. Not deathly ill, but dragged-down-with-fatigue, antsy, achy, coming-down-with-a-cold, unsettled, bone-weary sick; the kind of sickness that no one wants, especially day after day after day. Further, he was receiving maintenance chemo through the port in his neck.

On our last day in Tucson, Joe called and asked us to hurry to pick him up at the hospital. He told Jim to stay out front with the car while I came up to his room. After rushing to get him, however, I realized he wasn't really released because he hadn't had a visit from a doctor or nurse with final instructions or a release form that needed to be signed.

Still, Joe insisted he had been released and he was ready to go; he was dressed and had told someone to call for a wheelchair. I went up to his room, and while we waited together for the chair, Jim waited outside in the car. When the wheelchair arrived, Joe collapsed into it before the aide had set the brake. Joe fell to the floor onto the hip where his bone had been drilled to harvest stem cells.

I screamed, and people came running to help. Joe was livid because I created a scene. With as little fanfare as possible, we made our way to the elevator and down to the car. Joe was hungry for crab legs, so we found a local Joe's Crab Shack, and we ordered. We had barely started to eat our early lunch when the hospital called, insisting we bring Joe back to receive final instructions and sign release papers. We stuffed ourselves with crab legs and rushed back to the hospital.

The next morning, Joe went to his last appointment with his doctor, and Jim and I went to a nearby gym to walk on a treadmill before our endless hours of travel. Joe had agreed to meet us back at the apartment to say goodbye before he left. But after a short workout, Jim discovered that the wallet he'd left in the console of the car had been stolen. Our cash and all Jim's identification was gone.

We forgot about Joe as we rushed to the police station to report the theft. Someone had already charged almost $1,000 on Jim's card.

Joe must have returned to that empty apartment and assumed we'd gotten tired of waiting for him and left town. There was so much going on that we forgot to call him, and he didn't call us. Meanwhile, we found that without Jim's ID, we couldn't return the car to the airport or get on our plane or access our bank accounts. It was a busy day of cancellations before Jim remembered that he had an old military ID in his desk at home. He called our daughter, who found the ID card and sent it to us in overnight mail so that we could turn in the car, pay our bills, and get on an airplane. We finally left Tucson with a giant sigh of relief.

I don't know if we ever told Joe what happened that day. He must have had a terrible time going back to his Vegas apartment alone and taking care of himself. We didn't know if it had been deep-cleaned, how much time off he had, or what other obstacles lay ahead of him. He never mentioned any of it. The whole experience was exhausting for all of us.

16 The New Normal

After his stem cell transplant, Joe was supposed to wear a mask and gloves and avoid people until his immune system developed. He had headaches, chest congestion, low-grade fever, runny nose, fatigue, aches, pains, and every kind of symptom that announced, "You are getting sicker by the minute." It must have felt like being stabbed to death by knitting needles. He would have to fight every germ in his path for what probably felt like the rest of his life.

Just thinking about him made me tense and edgy, and that surely added to his stress. He couldn't stand to have anyone witness his discomfort, but it was obvious that he was not only suffering physically but he hated the treatment too. Multiple myeloma had come into his life the way a typhoon finds a man lost at sea.

Jim and I talked and prayed nonstop about his gambling and his refusal to discuss the disease that ruled his present and limited his future. That future was almost upon us, but we didn't know it. We were so concerned about his flagrant disregard for his physical condition that we never considered how short the *now* might be.

In some ways, his life with MM was similar to the car registration he let lapse. There was no real reason he didn't keep up with the administrative part of life. No drive-by shooting at the DMV made him avoid the place. Money couldn't have been the problem—he always worked, and he had jobs with titles like National Director of Sales. He only had himself to support, and his lifestyle was inexpensive. But he procrastinated until it was too late to avoid penalties and extra charges, and he dawdled after that.

He lived with MM the way he'd done all the rest of it. He ignored his disease as much as possible. He smoked and drank, and I think he was familiar with pot and painkillers. I doubt he would have done anything to knowingly damage his ability to concentrate because he had always spent inordinate amounts of time reading.

Doing the right thing has always been my intent. But my denial, lack of awareness, wishful thinking, and natural avoidance of conflict led me in circles when it came to my son. It was obvious that his lifestyle was self-destructive, and I saw him spiral down to a point that looked like no escape would be possible. Heavy clouds blocked the sun in that desolate territory. He needed to be saved, but I could not figure out how.

I was particularly disturbed to hear after the transplant that he'd decided to start over in the gaming industry. That made no sense to me at all. It wasn't my business, but of course I had an opinion . . . and an attitude.

When he first told us about the job, he had seemed happy that he could do it remotely, maybe even in North Carolina, but I didn't focus on that. I was hung up on the "enabling" aspect of the job. My disapproval was not a secret, and my attitude was unhelpful, unnecessary, and unkind.

You would think I'd have been thrilled about a job he could do remotely. Just think—he could live nearby! We could see him more often. He could even have a dog that we'd take care of if he wanted to go on a trip. There were so many advantages to this idea, but I did not acknowledge even one. Instead, I found a new worry—if he were nearby and became unable to manage his health care, we'd be expected to do it without notice or information. I astounded myself.

With all the criticism I had of my son, I was stunned, after he died, to find out about the exhaustive preparations he had made for his future success as an independent casino host. When he died, he left all the evidence of that proudly displayed on his kitchen counter—a new business license dated December 11, 2018; expensive new stationary; a list of clients impeccably organized by name, date, rating, and contact information; and finally, he'd left his unlocked computer and phone there for examination.

These may have been his final words to me because I had questioned how he could do this work, how he could go back to helping habitual gamblers access rewards for their patronage. I'm sure my questions seemed negative and judgmental. They were. It didn't occur to me at the time, but it does now.

I remember listening to him negotiating with a hotel one time because he thought they weren't treating a client properly. She was a little old blind lady, he said, and she needed more help. I should have realized that this job that I'd dismissed was important to him and other people too.

***

On the day I told Jim about this remote job and that Joe might want to come home, Jim said, "That's great! Don't say anything negative."

I responded by saying, "Well, no. I have to. We have to make some rules in the beginning, so we know what we're getting into."

I didn't want to jump into a big upheaval without knowing what was expected of me, and I didn't want to disappoint Joe and Jim and make myself miserable in the process. I had never felt so lost and unable to face the days ahead of me. I decided to try a new kind of counseling at our church called "listening prayer." It was supposed to help people who were stuck with a problem that had overtaken their lives. I definitely needed help, so I prayed and turned Joe's situation over to God. Then I waited for a response.

Nothing happened. My mind was an empty box.

I know God does not exist on my time, but I had trust and assurance. I had given the weight of Joe's problem to God, and with Him carrying it, I no longer felt desperate. I knew that I was not in control, that God was taking care of the things that happened in my life. Except this thing that was looming in front of us.

We knew Joe's job history, the series of losses and emotional body blows he'd been through, but we didn't consider him depressed. It's only from looking at pictures taken during that time that we've realized how utterly desolate he must have been feeling.

Jim would say, "We can't have him hanging around the house. We'll kill each other." Or "Just talk him into moving here, and we'll find an apartment for him. We'll pay for it, but don't tell him that. He needs to do something he wants to do, not something we've told him to do."

Jim wanted to deal with Joe in the moment, but I hated the idea of confrontation. I wanted to work out the problems ahead of time, so I sent Joe information on small houses and townhouses and condos near us. I mentioned that they cost half of what he was paying for rent in Vegas, but I didn't say we would pay for it. And he didn't respond. We were at a loss.

No matter what we considered doing, it seemed like another step into a rabbit hole of dead ends and wrong turns.

I knew that, statistically, more than 40 percent of patients with life-threatening chronic diseases become seriously depressed and need professional help. I was a patient myself; dealing with my heart transplant still required my full attention. There is no doubt that my problems and care impacted my family, including Joe.

Joe's diagnosis must have scared him; it certainly scared us. But instead of discussing our feelings with him, we remained frustrated and angry. His lack of concern and the secrecy he'd already shown would give us no chance to prepare ourselves for a future of caring for our son. I became so wrapped up in that fear that I missed the change in Joe. I'm sure it was there to see, but I didn't look.

Relentless pain and loss of function eventually defeat any person's positive mental attitude. And once a person's positive mindset changes to negative and hopeless, it's almost impossible to avoid the inevitable decline that can lead to the worst outcome of all, suicide ideation.

17 LIFE IN REMISSION

For years, Joe had insisted he didn't celebrate holidays. Christmas 2017 was drawing near, and he wasn't sure he would come home. I told him I was getting his nephews drones for Christmas, one for each of them so they could have a war. When Joe showed some interest, I told him I'd buy a drone for everyone so we could all participate. To my surprise, he decided to come home. I purchased eight drones, and included an invitation to the war on Christmas afternoon, in an empty field at the end of our street. I imagined it would be crazy, and I was not disappointed.

On Christmas morning, Joe was the first to finish constructing his drone. Triumphant, he galloped out the back door and chased it up and down the street faster than I'd seen him move in years. Back inside the house, we all joined the fray. One plane dive-bombed the staircase. Another had an audio feature that announced authentic *Star Wars* commands. The ragtag fleet swooped up to the high ceiling and dove onto the table. The dogs jumped and yapped, lampshades tipped, and a flying object hit the stove before crashing in the dining room.

The competition was exhilarating, and our fleet was in pieces before it was time for the war. Our grandchildren were giddy from the mayhem, adults were acting like kids, and we were having more fun than we had had in forever. But we couldn't escape reality for long.

Joe was still in remission from MM; he had suffered significant bone damage and should have been taking regular pain meds, yet after the chemo port had been surgically removed, we'd heard no further mention of medicines, or funds required for medical appointments. When I asked about it, he told me that the doctor who'd been with him since that first visit to the hospital had moved to a new practice.

My heart sank as I realized he probably wasn't seeing a doctor at all. But, like so many other things I suspected, I didn't ask. Even if I had known the truth, I don't know what I could have done that wouldn't have made him angry. Joe wasn't interested in my advice or my concern.

At one point before the holiday, he had called to tell me how much he was enjoying a beautiful day and a cup of gourmet coffee. With a happy sigh, he said, "I haven't had a five-dollar cup of coffee in forever."

"Why not?" I asked. Surely, he wasn't saying he couldn't afford one; that wasn't possible.

But he said, "Mom, I don't have two nickels to rub together."

I wanted to scream, *"Why?"* but I didn't. His problems did not make sense to me. And then he asked me how long I thought it had been since he had shut us out of his life.

I had no idea. "I don't know. Twenty years?" I answered. "Maybe more." As long as he was reflecting, I decided to ask something that had always puzzled me. "Do you remember when you were little and you refused to go to school?"

"Yeah."

"Why?" I asked.

"You didn't prepare me."

I didn't say the words that were on the tip of my tongue, but they were in my heart. *You didn't prepare me, either.*

I don't know where that conversation came from, but I can still hear the words we said to each other because they rang as true as a bell that marks the deep channel in a harbor.

***

Six months later, in the summer of 2018, we visited my brother and sister-in-law in Newport, Rhode Island. To our surprise, Joe joined us. He hated to travel and he complained nonstop about the crowded conditions, but he loved my brother, and he came.

I was concerned when I saw him because he had gained a lot of weight. He didn't mention pain during that visit, but his labored movements and heavy breathing made it obvious, and I worried about his lack of energy and future mobility.

We stayed at a hotel across from Easton's Beach, near a restaurant that specializes in lobster Benedict for breakfast. I tried not to indulge after having it once, but Joe convinced me to eat and be merry. He was good at that.

My brother knew Joe loved deep-sea fishing, and he wanted to make sure he caught a really big fish. Every morning, Barry picked Joe up and drove down to the boat at Long Wharf. However, every day presented a new problem—it was too windy, too choppy, too foggy.

On the final day, the sun was shining, the ocean was perfect, and out they went. Barry asked Joe if he wanted to drive the boat, and Joe raced toward the horizon, bouncing off waves and slamming over swells; he took the wind and spray in his face with a huge smile. Barry told me about it with great enthusiasm. Full speed had always made Joe happier than anything—even the huge bluefish they caught that day.

Later, we were walking single file on the path between our hotel and Flo's Clam Shack. I was in front of Joe, so I couldn't see his face. I wanted to talk to him about moving to North Carolina, and I said something like, "I wish you didn't live in a place where someone kills a whole bunch of innocent people at an outdoor concert. It would be nice if you lived closer, so you could have a relationship with your family and your nephews, all of whom would love to spend time with you."

Joe was silent for a minute before he answered. "I don't understand why they take a bunch of innocent people with them, but... but I can get down with suicide." He responded as though he had thought about suicide.

The conversation came out of the blue, and I had yet to learn that people don't speak idly about suicide. Any mention of it is a huge red flag and should be treated as an immediate danger. I can't imagine why I didn't react. It's another case of my brain not accepting what was happening.

When I could think again after Joe's death, I wanted to be of use to people who were in danger of killing themselves. I audited an advanced psychology class at East Carolina University, where graduate students who plan to be physicians and mental health professionals get experience dealing with people in crisis by answering the phone at the National Crisis Hotline. I was accepted as a volunteer, and I completed the training. I didn't take calls, but I listened in, and I role-played with my class.

When COVID-19 cancelled all in-person education, I had to stop. It was for the best though. Quarantine gave me time to recognize my own fragile mental state and my tendency to weep regularly, unexpectedly, about a zillion times a day. I was not ready to help someone else; like an airline passenger, I needed to connect my own oxygen mask first.

***

A month after vacationing with us in Newport, Joe called from Las Vegas to say his lease was expiring in September. He wondered if he should renew it for a few more months or come home to our guest room at the top of the stairs (his old room). I could have said, "That's wonderful! Of course we want you to come home"—but it wouldn't have been true. Every time he'd stayed with us as an adult, it was difficult for all of us.

So instead, I hesitated. "Uh . . . I'll have to talk to your father. At this point, Joe, I don't want to be in a bad situation with you. It's taken us years to get where we are, and I don't want to ruin the relationship we have now."

"I don't take up much space, Mom," he said, "and I don't make much noise. I don't even watch TV. I mostly stay in my room and work on my computer."

I didn't say the things I was thinking, like, *How long do you want to stay, and what do you expect of us?* I didn't even say what bothered me most: *What will be different this time? Because something needs to be different. We can't continue with you the way things are.*

No, I just said I had to talk to Jim. And then, when I did, my husband was pleased. "That's great!" he said.

I was obviously not enthused. "I told him I had to talk to you about it first."

Jim sighed. "Why do you always do that? Why do you worry about things that haven't happened yet? You know I'd be happy to pay his rent here in an apartment while he gets established."

"Well, then let me tell him that," I said.

"No," Jim replied. "He needs to know what he wants. When he figures that out, he'll do it. We can't give him what *we* want. He has to choose his own direction."

There were other reasons, too, that I was reluctant for him to live with us. First, he was a night owl, and we definitely were not. His day sleeping and night wandering drove us nuts. More importantly, however, Jim and I weren't the same people we'd been before we had accepted Christ.

Joe knew we were different, and I had an idea about how he would react when he had to deal with our new habits and lifestyle on a daily basis. I wanted religious freedom in my own home. Joe had already given us blowback about our church, just as he had received our negative opinions of his lifestyle. I was sure he would hate our new habit of turning Christian music up loud while we ate Egg McMuffins and watched gospel music on TV before going to church.

I expected him to realize all these things by osmosis, I guess, because I didn't bring them up or explain how I felt. Instead, I let the subject slide—one week, two. Finally, he called to ask what we'd decided, and I told him we were against him coming home.

"You waited two weeks to tell me NO?" he protested.

"I told you I wanted to talk to your father about it, and I did." I scrambled to find a logical reason for my delay. "We're going to be putting the house on the market soon. We're on the list for one of those senior communities. They're going to build a house for us."

Joe was not impressed. "Haven't I told you not to do that?" he growled. "Places like that are rip-offs. They take your money and use it or lose it. They'll be bankrupt by the time you need them to take care of you."

I didn't like the kitten telling the cat what to do. He was asking to live with us, but he was acting like the boss of our home. It was infuriating, and I was provoked.

I said, "You don't even like us, Joe."

"I love you, Mom." His words were instant, like the truth. Natural. I was shocked speechless. It had been so long since I had heard that, so long since he had said it, that I could not speak, but inside I was screaming, *Then tell me why you are killing yourself and forcing us to watch?*

Jim and I had been intentionally saying, "I love you," at the end of our conversations with our son for years. It always seemed to catch him off-guard. His response, "See ya," was like a slap in the face with a wet towel.

"Mom?" Joe, on the other end of the phone, heard only my silence, and it lasted a long time. "Why aren't you saying anything?"

"I have no words." It was true. I tried to find some, but my mouth was not connected to my brain.

"You always have words."

But I didn't.

After what seemed like an eternity, he said, "Okay, goodbye."

I thought a lot about that phone call. I still do. I wanted to send a card that said, "I'm sorry. I do love you, and I love you unconditionally." In fact, sometimes, I thought I had sent a card. But I didn't.

Instead, I told myself it didn't matter, that it wasn't a big deal, that he must not have thought those words were important. That's why he never said them himself; he didn't care. To some people, *I love you* is a forever-unto-death statement. Some people say *I love you* all the time and don't mean it. Others, whether they mean it or not, never say it.

But I didn't change my answer. I didn't tell him to come home.

18 The Land of Maureen

Many years ago, I was diagnosed with breast cancer, and Jim prayed for me nonstop while I was sick. When I was finally pronounced cancer-free, he wanted to go to church to thank God. We went on an Easter Sunday, and afterward, Jim told me he'd been born again. I didn't understand what he was talking about, but he had no other explanation for the change in his heart. I was skeptical of his sudden conversion and was not afraid to complain about it to the kids and other people. Jim responded by continuing to pray for me. Time did not change his fervor. After a while, I became used to the new Jim.

Meanwhile, the medication I had taken for breast cancer manifested its "possible side effect" of heart failure. The possibility hadn't mattered to me when I had cancer. Cancer should be eradicated immediately, I'd thought. Heart failure . . . that would take a long time to be really bad. And of course, I didn't expect it to happen to me.

I managed it for years with medication and lifestyle changes. I was a model patient. My health was a big focus in our lives, and I managed to go many years before I needed a heart transplant. But by the time I was sixty-nine, I was in heart failure. My advanced age, uncommon blood type, and the fact that I had been managing my health well for so long made me an unlikely candidate for a transplant. That was okay with me; I was terrified.

The doctors told me I would never be called, but on Labor Day weekend in 2011, I was the only person within 400 miles of a donor who had the same blood type, tissue match, and physical size as me. Terrified and thrilled, we rushed to the hospital in Washington, D.C.

I was blessed to receive the heart of a beautiful, twenty-six-year-old mother from Kenly, North Carolina. While I wrestled with the guilt of living, the surgery was deemed successful. Five days later, a large hematoma caused my lung to collapse, and my chest cavity filled with blood. Doctors told Jim the safest thing to do was reopen my chest and see what could be done. I was put into a coma and the surgeon repaired several leaks.

Days later, when I awakened, I was different. Like Jim, I had come to Christ. God had given me a new life, a chance to do over what had been done. A chance to do it better. I embraced the opportunity, but as you know by reading this, I am still very much a work in progress. I am better than I used to be—but not as good as I would wish.

Jim and I are both different than we were. Not in a bad way, but the change is unmistakable. Our children were already grown when this happened, and our new spirituality surprised them in an eye-rolling kind of way. I understand. I knew how they felt. I had complained about Jim.

Children expect their parents to forever remain the familiar people they grew up with. Having a sick mother who needed a heart transplant was scary enough for my family; the new me was unpredictable. At first, like most transplant patients, I was on large doses of prednisone, which causes emotional storms of tears and anger... and a big puffy face like a squirrel with her cheeks full of nuts.

In addition, the new me values my gift of life in a way that is impossible to explain. I would never choose to knowingly eat or drink something that was not good for my little Chickadee heart. My choices are not made out of discipline; I have the privilege of being alive. There is no greater motivation. God does not owe me good health because I live a healthy life. I am abundantly blessed.

The new me was an evangelist and a health nut. God's gift of a new heart awakened me to the serious responsibility I had to take care of my body, the "temple of the Holy Spirit." I'd never known that before. My vigilance was what I owed my donor family for their gift. I became very serious about maintaining my health with good habits. This was another surprise for my children.

It probably took a year for me to settle down. During that time, I was a big job for everyone. My family has never complained, but I can be honest—I'm still a big job.

But even though I was a Christian now, and even though I was constantly aware of my health and life choices, I was still Maureen. I still had to be in control, only now I was more confident in my choices.

I had literally spent years in turmoil about my son's lack of concern for his health, his employment, his finances, his future, and the complete disorganization of his life. Why should I stop trying to manage him now?

Of course, my worry hadn't altered the trajectory of his path—in fact, it had done more to ruin our relationship and deprive him of a place that was safe from criticism than it had to help him.

I had never acknowledged that his life was his and that he was free to live it according to his choices. I had never considered that I had no real power to change who he was or who he wanted to be. And I had never recognized that he might be too depressed to pull himself together.

In the land of Maureen, where I assumed responsibility for everything as though I were the Almighty God himself, I ran in circles like a hamster in a wheel, refusing to relinquish my obsession of fixing my son so that he could be more like I wanted him to be. More like someone he didn't want to be.

Even if I'd had any right to complain about his life, my "fixing" never included any practical steps. I just spouted complaints.

I knew Joe was smart, capable, and ahead of the crowd in terms of his mental and physical gifts. I assumed he had the ability to live the life he wanted. I thought the day would come when he would find God and get it together—and it was impossible to reconcile my opinion of my wonderful son with the choices he made. Still, every time I was ready to throw in the towel, something would renew my hope for him.

Did you notice how many times you just read the pronouns *I* and *my*? It confounds me to realize how controlling I sound and how I never learned from my failures.

Back when he was building the call center in Vegas in 2008, Joe had asked us to cover his rent, car payment, and cell phone for six months. "Well, if we are going to do that for you," I said, "I'd like you to do something for us."

"What?"

"Go to church!"

To my surprise, he agreed. Our neighbor knew someone who had started a church near Joe, and I passed on the recommendation.

I can't believe I actually thought I could change my son's life by getting him to attend a religious service. As though the God of all creation didn't know where my son was or what he needed.

I obviously did the wrong thing while intending to do the right thing—I believed that God would change Joe's heart if I could just get him in the building. Now I know that God doesn't swoop down from heaven and attack people who wander into a church. People have free will; they have to make their own choices, good and bad. God didn't create a bunch of robots to hang around and worship Him because He said they have to. He loves us, but we must invite Him into our lives.

God doesn't want people who already believe in Him to try to force others to believe the same way, either. He wants us to be so much like Him that other people will recognize that something is missing in their lives without Him. The huge benefit of having a personal relationship with God is serenity. There's a recognizable fullness to life when it's lived based on His love. That's what people recognize after choosing Him. It's what they should see in us.

We are all sinners, but when we look up to heaven and ask God to come into our lives and direct our paths, He opens His arms and welcomes us in. He certainly doesn't need a meddling, controlling person like me to step in, to judge, and to get in the way of someone else's free will. Not even my son's. What I did was doomed, and it created a disastrous situation that lasted much longer than the six months of financial help Joe received.

God didn't need me to force His divine intervention. My hubris offended both Joe and God, and it still embarrasses me. Neither of them asked me to be in charge; they had their own relationship. There is no doubt that I am a slow learner. But I also have no doubt that they are together now.

The land of Maureen is a place of constant learning.

19 Perception and Reality

There's no explanation for how a good day becomes a bad day, like the day Joe said, "I'm wondering what to do when my lease expires. I was thinking about the room at the top of the stairs."

Why I didn't say, "Come home," I will never know.

I'm sad today because Joe might have wanted to turn back the clock and be different. I wish I could do that too. I also wish I had bought him the cocker spaniel puppy he'd wanted one Christmas. Did I ever give him what he wanted without first putting in my two cents? In the end, it was as though he no longer expected or wanted to enjoy anything. He had already checked out. I don't think he ever expected me to tell him not to come home, but that's what I did. And I still can't believe it.

There was a news story in July 2021 about a grandfather who held his grandchild while she stood on the railing of a cruise ship to look at the sea. The child slipped out of his grasp and fell to her death. When I heard that story, I had a gut-wrenching reaction. I knew how that grandfather had felt.

Joe was fond of saying, "Perception is reality." His perception might have been his reality, but when I put mine beside his, I became confused. The way he treated us made me wonder if he cared about us at all. He always seemed angry with us, though there was never an acknowledgment of any problem. It didn't matter what we said, the force of his anger would push us away. Then he'd leave us, discarded in a silent place, until he decided to get over it. Or until he needed money.

It's sad to hold on to pain or to be in a relationship with someone who does. Joe and I both cherished our suffering. But if just one person changes, everything can change. And after counseling at church and practicing "listening prayer," my mind and heart began to change.

I gave my son to God, and I prayed for direction—for a clear indication of what I should do. As I waited for God to give me an answer, the weight of the problem was lifted from my shoulders. I no longer felt the doom of a threatening cataclysm. I really believed God would take care of it, maybe not in my idea of a timely fashion, but surely in God's time.

Although it was obvious we were in some kind of crisis, I washed my hands of it and turned away from the debacle. I now realize that when you turn a problem over to God, you should also make a plan. I could have tried to take Joe to a therapist or counselor. I don't think he would have cooperated, but I could have tried to get him some insurance, a doctor, the medication he no doubt needed, or the testing he probably should've had.

I could have offered to get a lawyer to help him apply for benefits. Many people need a lawyer to help with an early Social Security application. I could have suggested that he look into and compare the benefits North Carolina offered to those available in Las Vegas. I could have indicated my willingness to help with a solution for what was an existential problem. I could have opened my mouth and told him how I felt.

Why didn't I think of that? Why didn't he?

And then I looked at the facts in front of me. I didn't know where he worked. I didn't know his boss's name or contact information. I hadn't even known Joe's insurance policy numbers when he went through his stem cell transplant. We were there with him the whole time, but he refused us permission to talk to his doctor. How likely was it that he would suddenly do as we asked with his health, much less the administrative chores of his life?

Maybe this time, he was finally in such a tough situation that he would have appreciated some help. But he didn't seem to care or want us to care . . . even though we were his backup plan and we *did* care.

Every year, during the New Year holiday, Jim reviews and updates our personal financial information and sends a copy to each of our kids. In case of emergency, they know where our will is, how to access an account to get cash, whom to call about our funeral arrangements, what's changed in our assets, what our passwords are, etc. Having a plan is important to us.

I think Joe didn't want us to know his personal information because he knew we would be disappointed; it must have been important to keep us in the dark about his screwed-up finances, because there was nobody to blame but himself.

We never did figure out what triggered the problems he lived with, but we knew he'd started out in a good place. He had a degree from a good school, no school loan, no car loan, a healthy retirement account, and excellent health. He was good-looking, smart, funny, and he got along well with people. We were proud of him. We *still are* proud of him—he was a terrific person, and there is a huge hole in our universe without him.

When they took his stem cells, they harvested enough for two transplants. Three bags of frozen cells waited at the University of Arizona in Tucson. Sometime after his death, I called and spoke to someone there about this, hoping that the institution would give his DNA to ancestry.com. I would like his information in that vast database. I don't want it to be as though he didn't exist. I wanted him to continue on a family tree with children and a wife; those things will never be, but he was here—and I don't want our family to forget him.

I'm sorry every day—sorry that I didn't know what to do, didn't find out what to do, and most of all, sorry that Joe is gone.

I do believe, though, that if God's plan was for me to take care of Joe, he would still be here and our relationship would be working. God would have made sure that happened. That's what He does—He makes possible what is, for us, impossible. But you have to believe in change, initiate the change, and own the commitment to change.

I could have made the time to have some heart-to-heart talks with our son, but I didn't. Frankly, he wasn't interested in the kind of life we wanted for him—an ordinary life where you get a job, get married, and have a family. It's kind of funny, actually, because when he was about ten years old, he had a dream that he had twin boys and named one of them Adam. He told me he was going to have five children, and on some level, I guess I expected that to happen.

It was much easier for all of us to wallow in our perceptions and complain about unmet expectations than it was to acknowledge and deal with the reality that was staring us in the face.

20 Bargaining

What did Joe do with the money he was making? What had put him so far in credit card debt? I assumed it all went for gambling, but I had no proof. Whatever it was, he obviously didn't manage his money well. Without even trying, I can come up with so many different ways he *could've*, *should've*, and *would've*... But what do I know?

And then I think about what I could've done. What I should've done but didn't. But I can't do that any longer. Whenever I think about what might have happened if I had done this or that, I find myself back in the bargaining stage of grief.

It seems like no matter how far forward I manage to go in this journey, I somehow end up bargaining again.

The way Joe chose to run his life didn't work. Repeatedly, for twenty, maybe thirty years. But those were things his parents couldn't fix.

He'd been blessed with good health, but he treated his body as though it was worthless. We who loved him wore ourselves out worrying. It didn't occur to me that depression might have been the cause, but now, with open eyes, I recognize that the malady had existed in my father and other family members. It should have been obvious... Why didn't I address that? I was in denial.

Joe had good times with friends who sang karaoke and played cards, met him at bars and talked all night long. I didn't know him in those moments, but I'm glad he had them.

I think of how miserable he must've been when the bills piled up. It had to be awful, having to start over so many times in different industries. How many times did he learn everything there was to learn about a new product, and how many customer bases did he build? But then I remember his excitement at each new challenge and the loss of interest as the challenge waned. Maybe that up-and-down was just who he was.

What if Joe was doing exactly what he wanted to do? What if he was making his choices based on his knowledge of his condition, taking the risks associated with an unhealthy diet and lifestyle because he wasn't worried about the long-term consequences. He was dealing with a short timeline. He was an adult, created by God, loved by God, allowed free will by God.

Joe said he could sell anything—and really, he could. He did. He even sold temporary buildings, the kind constructed at the site of major disasters or used for hospitals or restaurant additions. I marveled when I heard him rattling off the measurements of a clamshell entrance.

Our son had all the gifts of the Irish—especially blarney. He made a great dinner companion because he was interested in so many things. He could find common ground to engage almost anyone. He was hilarious when it came to current events and pompous political figures. The election hysteria he described was outrageous, unbelievable, incredible, and true; there was no nuance that he missed. He kept us laughing, as though the absurdity of life was something he didn't want us to miss. He had a wicked sense of humor and a clever wit. Every time I see something unbelievable on the news or in the paper, I want to call to hear his reaction. We all miss talking to him; he was such an active listener.

And then I realize how much of that part of him I missed or sidestepped ... because I was so focused on what I perceived as his shortcomings.

Someone needed to hold an intervention with him. Of course, I can't imagine myself or anyone else, no matter how professional, flying to Vegas and confronting him. What would we have said?

"What's going on here? I'm worried about where you are and where you're going. Let me take you to a doctor—one you'll allow to speak to me about your condition. Tell me why you are broke even with a job where you're the national sales director. Let me take over your finances—you don't manage your life well, and not only is it killing you, Joe, it's killing us to watch it happen. None of this makes any sense. You need to stop hurting yourself and those who care."

But how do you make that happen? When someone you love is getting close to the end of his rope and you know it's time to get him out of that situation, how do you do it?

We were in a boat with Joe, and the current was propelling us toward a cliff. I could hear the roar of the waterfall through the trees. I was terrified he would die from multiple myeloma or related problems, or alcohol or pain meds, all without telling the people who could help. I should have picked up an oar or started the engine.

But instead, we pretended there was a different reality than the one he inhabited. We told ourselves he would spend a happy Christmas at a friend's house where he'd play games and laugh with people he cared about. We even provided the dinner to help that happen.

And that's what he did. Right up to the point where he bought a gun with his Christmas money and shot himself.

How am I supposed to accept the fact that I'm the one who told him not to come home? That I'm the one who sent the money he used to purchase the gun?

If I could erase it all, if he could come home tomorrow, I still don't know what we would do to make him go to a doctor. How we'd find out about his insurance or get him signed up for Obamacare. It seemed impossible to do anything without his cooperation, but in our wildest dreams, we never considered trying to take away his ability to make decisions for himself.

Unfortunately, that doesn't make me feel any better because, now that the unspeakable has happened, I realize how impaired he was. Joe wasn't just dealing with an incurable disease, chronic fatigue, and constant bone pain. He was dealing with the trauma of suffering alone, of keeping his problems a secret.

Hiding his situation and his emotional pain might have been the heaviest burden of all. I am sorry. I wish I had sent him a card that said, "I love you unconditionally, today and every day, and I always will."

A Letter to Joe

May 1, 2019

Four months have passed since your death, Joe, and today has been hard. This morning, I was in tears thinking of you. We didn't realize that although change is as necessary as oxygen, you were too burned-out to do it on your own. We now see that you were worn out from dealing with your disease, from people telling you what to do, and from working hard to stay afloat and not having enough money to survive independently. There was no hope on your horizon.

Whatever help we provided in the past had only enabled you to continue in the status quo; no one ever did anything to solve the root of your problems. And that's on you. At this point, I feel sure that what you needed was counseling, medication, structure, activity, accountability, and a support system to help you keep your spirits up. There was nothing in your life to look forward to.

You said you liked the Las Vegas lifestyle, but I don't think you would have said that in the end. It offered no security, no future, and it was killing you. Dad and I both agree that a check might have changed your decision to die. We wish we had tried something, *anything*. But I think you might have had this on your mind for a while and it was going to be the eventual outcome, even if you'd stayed with us to have a respite from living expenses.

Of course, the companies that offer a "new start" would have been there to help you down the same path to financial ruin once again. Our mailbox is full of offers for cars and credit cards. I charged your phone the other day and found "the quote you requested" to lease a brand-new Lincoln Continental.

It could have just been aggressive marketing, but maybe you had plans we didn't know about. Maybe those plans required time in our house.

I am definitely bargaining again.

We would have done anything for you, Joe. We would've had you on the next plane. I think you didn't want to deal with us; you didn't want to see us look at each other and know we were thinking, "This can't be our son. It's not possible." You didn't want to admit to yourself or to us that you were a step away from losing the ability to call the shots in your own life. You wanted to be in control of medical intervention and your own physical and mental state. You must have believed it was easier to die than to seek help, any help, but especially ours. And that hurts.

I think that's all for today. I look forward to seeing you when we don't have this problem. I hope you are at peace, and, of course, I hope you have a dog. It would be good for you. I miss you, Joe.

Love, Mom

21 What We Didn't Know

I recently found a book in the trunk of my car; it was Ruth Bell Graham's *Prodigals and Those Who Love Them*. In it, she discussed how angry she was with her son when he was lost in a lifestyle she didn't approve of. She compares her anger to Moses's fury when he came down from the mountain with the Ten Commandments and found his tribesmen worshipping a golden cow. Moses was so furious, he threw the tablets down and broke them.

I found myself carrying similar anger toward the son who had not turned out the way I wanted—yet I was not the same mother Joe had grown up with. I was this new goody-two-shoes who, like the Pharisees in the Bible, looked askance at my son who was addicted to a bad lifestyle. I carried the same withering self-righteousness.

I thought Joe was suffering because of his poor choices, and I tried to force him to see that, to make him want to change. After all, change is self-generated. But who was I to judge? I had my own failures to deal with. What I should have done is pray for the grace I needed to reach out like Christ, to offer love, and to ask forgiveness for judging. Instead, I judged.

I doubt Joe is angry with me, but I think he knows I wasn't in a good place either. No matter how I try to explain, excuse, or justify myself, the truth is that even if we could not have lived together peacefully, home is somewhere you should always be welcome. My expectations and his habits were diametrically opposed, but a mother's love should be as safe and reliable and unchanging as a port in a storm.

Now that I've had a son with suicide sickness, I have learned that serious depression and PTSD happen on a regular basis to people who have chronic, fatal diseases. It's not the experience of receiving a diagnosis like multiple myeloma that causes hopelessness or thoughts of suicide. It is the subsequent grinding down of physical, mental, and spiritual resilience by endless medical intervention and the person's own recognition that a cure is not a goal or even part of the plan. With the realization that a chronic, fatal condition cannot be overcome or ignored, the effort to exist can become unsustainable. Hope and a positive attitude are fantasies of the past.

Joe was unemployed, and he lived alone without a support system. He knew he wasn't going to recover from his disease. And, no doubt, he had considered all his options. Looking back, I do not think he was capable of enacting change; I think he had run out of energy and time.

My son didn't need me to tell him what was wrong or try to fix it or give him a pep talk. He needed me to accept him as he was and where he was. He needed comfort without judgment. He needed unconditional, Christlike love.

Instead, I was angry. I made it about me by assuming he didn't care that he had broken my heart by choosing a horrible life. I thought he was a good and loving person who had intentionally denied himself a wife and family, the love of a pet, and a future with financial security, because he would rather be free to kill himself with unhealthy addictions. I thought that, if he had just turned to God, it would make a huge difference in his life.

Actually, now I think he did have God in his life. I don't know if it took being at the bottom, but that is where many people turn to God, and that's where Joe was.

Addictions and breakdowns exist in all families. Even when there was only one family, Cain killed Abel. In retrospect, we should have been aware of the likelihood that we would have a child who would deal with addiction or depression or any of a plethora of other hereditary issues. The family of man battles thousands of fatal diseases and mental disorders, why would ours be exempt? It wasn't—both Joe's grandfather and his great-grandfather had killed themselves.

Even though multiple myeloma had changed the probability of Joe having a normal life-span, we foolishly remained fixated on his gambling and drinking, as though his behavior was likely to ruin his chance to enjoy his mythical sunset years.

We never expected perfection or instant maturity; most people experience a few hiccups on the way to adulthood. Nor did we worry that we might be modeling aberrant behavior to our children; we thought we were fine. We thought they would adopt our work ethic so they could afford the life they had become accustomed to. We were confident we knew what was best for them.

We didn't know what we didn't know.

It's funny how events from the past pop up in my memory to illustrate a lesson I didn't learn when I was supposed to. My grandson's school called me once to ask me to bring his lunch because he'd forgotten it. I was out, so I went to McDonald's for a Happy Meal. As I sat in the lunchroom with Ryan and his classmates, I became self-conscious because he had McDonald's while the rest of the kids at our table had little brown paper bags.

I assumed they might be jealous, and I said, "I'm sorry Ryan doesn't have his regular lunch." A little girl replied, "My mother says we have enough money to buy good food instead of McDonald's." I had to laugh.

What a brilliant mom. I wish I had known what to say when my son was little. I wish I had said, "Joe, there is nothing worth killing yourself over."

Jim and I shared the same strict religious background and the strong belief that God was in our lives. We believed that raising good people was a parent's most important job, and we did that. The religious instruction we received as children had sustained us through difficult times, but then we drifted away. There was a lot of controversy in our church, and I may have used it as an excuse to leave. I thought we'd be just fine with bedtime prayers and grace at meals.

I did not expect to be "born again," and I certainly didn't expect my sudden change to cause my children to compare me to the church lady on *Saturday Night Live*. When I realized that the Bible was a two-thousand-year-old historical record of man, I was so fired up, I tried to force-feed my adult children the wonder of those ancient words. Since then, I have calmed down, and they have gotten used to me. We are in a good place.

I didn't know what was missing in my life before I found God, but at this point, I've received so much peace and spiritual healing that I cannot imagine living without Him. I definitely see the advantage now of raising children with the knowledge of a loving, forgiving God who accepts and loves them without reservation. As humans, we should treat others as we would like to be treated, without judgment or condemnation, and leave it to God to sort things out.

In the end, the most important thing our children should know is that they need never be alone in the world—God, who forgives their transgressions no matter what, loves them and does not leave them. There are a plethora of things in the world that we do not know or understand, but we can count on God to solve the unsolvable problems out there.

As a child, my fear of going to hell for a small infraction like not wearing a hat to church or eating meat on Friday left me more afraid of priests and eternal damnation than comforted by Christ's presence and forgiveness. I did not understand how Christ could have died for my sins before I'd been born to commit them. I hadn't been taught to worship; I'd been raised to attend. As an adult, I used religion's blind eye to its own moral failures (like pedophilia) as an excuse to give up on organized religion completely. Now we are born again, of all things, and I count my lack of familiarity with the Bible as the greatest failure of my education. It is just amazing.

I had no idea that I was leaving God out of my life while I was doing it. Neither do I have words to describe my own spiritual journey because I am still on it. Since I didn't have my own personal relationship with Jesus Christ, I had no idea what that was like to show it to my children. My goal was just to raise kids who were honest and kind, and I feel blessed by how wonderful they are and how gracious they have been to Jim and me as our focus has changed.

22 Trust in the Lord

Recently, I reflected on that little voice in my biblical dream the night before Joe died. I've realized since then that there are many places in the Bible where someone had a troubling dream about a future event. The purpose of such dreams was to foretell or forewarn someone of an upcoming event. Some would call my dream a prophecy, and I would agree.

I believe the little voice in my prophetic dream foretold Joe's death to prepare me for the terrible days that were to follow. I woke from that dream with a sustaining message—*Trust in the* LORD. *Lean not on your own understanding.* There were days when those words were the only thing that got me through.

I know God can take an imperfect vessel like me and transform it to His use. When I released Joe into God's hands that night, I said I would never second-guess Him. I don't think I'm second-guessing Him now, but I do think I'm at a better level of understanding. I wasn't supposed to understand—I was just supposed to step out in faith. I needed the conviction that Christ has when He forgives us.

A person has to be true to himself, and I have to be true to myself. I realize now, as I go forward, that I was not as *Christian* as I wanted to be or as I thought I was. Joe had a fatal disease and knew he would not live long. He saw no purpose in changing his lifestyle. That made it stupid for me to fuss about it.

I wasn't "in the moment" at all the last year or two that he was here, and I haven't been in the right moment for all these pages of excuses.

It's too late to carry on about what I could have done and didn't do. It's time to let that go and do what I can. I was responsible for the child created by God and given into my care as a baby. I wanted him to be happy and grateful to God and comfortable in his life. I wanted Joe to be surrounded by a family that loved him. I wanted him to have a wife and children to carry on after him and to keep his memory alive. Of course, that might have been partially to validate my own idea of how life should be lived, but if Joe had wanted that life, he could have had it.

It is also obvious that I could have been more accepting of the life he did choose, and I should not have spent my time judging him. Joe made his choices from different experiences than the ones I'd had. He was intelligent enough to know what he wanted, and what he was willing to do in order to get it.

I love my son, and I'm sorry he was in such physical, spiritual, and emotional pain that he did not want to live any longer. He was a sensitive soul, and I believe he felt things more deeply than I do. But the only way I can get past his final decision is through those words God set in my heart the night of my dream. *Trust in the* Lord. *Lean not on your own understanding.*

Jim and I traveled to Israel in 2005, where we walked on the Via Dolorosa and visited the places where Jesus had spoken. The olive trees, the garden of Gethsemane, the place where Pontius Pilate washed his hands—they exist exactly as they are described in the Bible. Seeing them was believing. Seeing them was a life-changing experience. Remembering those things that had been prophesied about Jesus centuries before they happened has strengthened my faith through the years and brought me closer to Him.

But faith can be hard to sustain after an experience like this. Joe's death changed us to the core. It happened in a minute, but going forward is taking the rest of our lifetime. Losing a member of your nuclear family alters the future forever. Every phone call has less news; there is an empty chair at every celebration.

We are like a tree, planted as a seed, watered and fed for a while, then ignored or attacked by cicadas. We grow, bloom, and mature, and no one notices us for a long time. Then the wind blows us sideways—an internet installation severs an important root; a drought is followed by a flood—and suddenly our tree exists only in early pictures of our yard, when we remember our swing that took us so high that the rope went slack for a moment before bringing us back.

I see Joe in pictures, and I wonder why it was not possible to stop him. Why did he do what he did?

After all this time, I still struggle to accept the limits of what I could have done. The problem wasn't money. The fact that we threw money at Joe's problems may have allowed them to continue. Still, I never could have slept at night if I had turned my back and left him to flounder. Fear made me transfer money to his account. It wasn't that I believed money could fix him; I hoped it would delay an implosion until I could figure out what to do.

At the same time that I worry about these things, I am becoming less codependent. As I have finally accepted the fact that I could not have single-handedly fixed my son or my relationship with him, I am learning to lean more heavily on God. A lot.

Surprisingly, my sense of peace remains with me. These days, I'm not walking the floor unable to sleep, and I'm not unsettled. I have confidence about myself and where Joe is. Every time I question God, I hear the words, "Trust in the Lord. Lean not on your own understanding."

So I believe and I stand firm on those instructions. I am trying to let go of things I cannot change. I am trying to let go of my unforgiveness. Like all my efforts, the secret is in getting back on the horse when I fall off. And every time, I come back to that divine assurance.

"Trust in the Lord and lean not on your own understanding" (Proverbs 3:5). I am grateful for those words. I could not have lived all this time without them.

23 Ever-Present Grief

There is something about grief that surprises me: it's always there and always here. I can be going along just fine, having a wonderful day, when suddenly something unexpected catches my eye or my heart, and I am back in the darkness of grief. It's not constant anymore, which is encouraging. But it's there.

Out of the blue, I think about Joe's last birthday when he was all alone—and again I am horrified at myself and the excuses I gave for my lack of action. I just wanted someone else to take charge. I had worried about Joe for so long. We had asked for prayers so many times. We had turned to God for help. But we *did* nothing.

And we pretended that everything was okay long beyond the time we believed it. Nothing was okay, but I blamed Joe for making it impossible to be any better.

God says have mercy, but I didn't have mercy. I lost patience, and I am so sorry. If there was one thing I would change, it would be my lack of empathy. I grieve for the attitude I gave my son. I grieve because I know I let myself get so far into my anger and impatience that I forgot the good things about him. I focused so hard on my worry and frustration that I forgot how funny he was.

As the years pass, I am remembering less about my worry and more about how much fun Joe was. Not just what he said, but how and when he said it. He was a charmer who often disarmed us with his sense of humor focused like a laser on pompous, self-inflated egos. We had the best conversations back then. He was so intelligent, well-read, and up to date that it was a treat to be in his sphere of phone pals. He made us laugh at ordinary things, and he had an uncanny way of identifying the absurdity of a situation. He laughed at himself and the way life turns things upside down, no matter what the original plan.

It's nice to remember the good, to focus on the happy moments. The sad ones, the bad ones...they're there, but they serve no purpose, and they no longer loom as large.

I do regret that I did nothing to prepare my children for life when it came to Jesus. Being a good person isn't enough and being honest isn't enough—not when the real problems of life arrive. Children need absolute trust in the divine love and mercy of a forgiving God. I did not educate Joe in a way that would have helped him with this, and I was not a good model of the behavior of Christ.

I pray for him and apologize to him every time I miss him, and that turns out to be every day. I know death is inevitable, but I wake every morning hoping to find this was all a bad dream. And I pray that no other parent has to lose their child to suicide.

24 Island Time

According to Jesus himself, the number one rule is to love God above all else, and the number two rule is to love others as you love yourself and forgive them as God forgives you. Together, they become what we know as the Golden Rule—*Do unto others as you would have them do unto you.* Love people as they are, unconditionally. Don't judge or you'll be judged. I failed at following that rule.

What a waste I made of my relationship with my son. What a disappointment I became to myself. If I didn't believe in God's forgiveness, I would be lost. But thank God, I do. And because of it, I am found. What happened to my son taught me that I am not qualified to judge anyone. I am confident that God and Joe are together and they have both forgiven me.

Forgiveness is the key to peace. When I was angry with Joe, I thought I had forgiven him. I said it again and again. But saying it doesn't make it true, and every time he failed to do what I wanted, I was right back at unforgiveness. It didn't matter how many times I *said* I wasn't angry. It didn't matter how many times I pronounced myself "over it." It doesn't matter how many times I thought it was true. That's not how it works. If I am confronted with the source of my anger and I feel angry again, I have not yet forgiven.

I'll be honest; it is hard to forget the anger. But I will try again and again until it is fully true. And I will take action to make it so. As I think of Joe, I have realized that he probably received very few random acts of kindness. I've decided to pray for people when I see their need, and I do that to honor my son's spirit.

I had occasion recently to stop at the shoe repair shop. The old man there is on oxygen, and he asked me to go behind the counter myself to get my repaired shoe. Unexpectedly, I found myself asking, "Are you feeling bad? Would you like me to pray for you?"

His eyes opened wide, and he nodded. Without an idea of what to do next, I put my hand on his arm and began to pray. "Thank you, God, for your blessings. I'm standing here with a man who has worked hard his whole life." I asked the man his name, then continued: "Marvin is tired, and he is hurting. Please raise his spirits and give him peace and rest. You've said that where two or more are gathered in your name, they can ask anything—and we are here, Lord, to ask for relief for Marvin's pain. He needs your touch. Let us pray together in the holy name of Jesus, amen." Someone walked into the store then, and I left. I felt good, and remembering Joe felt good.

Later that day, John, the man who cuts the grass for my neighbor, was leaning on the fence between our properties. He called me over to tell me that he'd been in the hospital. He wanted to tell me how bad his feet hurt. I went into the house to get him a few bottles of water and a box of candy I had planned to give someone for Easter.

Returning, I said, "Would you like me to pray for your feet, John?" He nodded, so I did. "Dear God, please bless John and bring healing to his feet. John is a good man who believes in your power to relieve the pain his feet are suffering. Thank you in the name of your Son, Jesus, amen."

Afterward, I walked into my house and thanked God for the courage He had given me to step out of my comfort zone and use His name with others, inspired by Joe. I intend to do this more often, and I hope to become more comfortable doing it. But it doesn't matter if I am ever comfortable; I would rather live with discomfort than be blind to the people who might like to hear a kind word.

Not long ago, I was out running errands and got caught at a traffic light. A man was standing in the median beside my window with his back toward me. His bowed head was covered by a too-large, wrinkled hoodie that looked like it had probably been slept in. I was stopped closest to the traffic light, and I felt safe in assuming this man was probably a drug addict working his usual territory.

Still, my conscience made me open my purse to see what kind of little money I had. Oddly enough, Jim had just given me fifty dollars, so I had two bills—the fifty and a one-dollar bill. I looked at them, and a thought went through my mind. *If Joe were here, he would want me to give this man the fifty.*

I put the fifty in my left hand and opened the window to address the man's back. "Hey," I said.

When he turned around and came toward me, I read his sign. "God bless you and your family."

I had expected, "Homeless, please help. Will work for food."

"What's wrong with you?" I asked.

"I'm having a tough time. I've applied for several jobs, but I'm still waiting to hear back."

His clothes were a mess, but his eyes were clear, his voice was strong, and he had a beautiful smile. I handed him the bill and said, "My son had a tough time, too."

"How's he doing now?" he asked.

"He killed himself," I answered. "Don't do that."

"I'm so sorry," he said. Then he noticed that the bill in his hand was a fifty, and his eyes widened; his face actually transformed.

"Are you sure you can afford to do this?" He tried to hand it back to me.

"Yes. I want you to have it."

"My name is Jason, and I want to pray for you. What's your name?"

We were at the four-way stop in our town's busiest intersection, and the light had changed.

"Maureen," I said, and he repeated it incorrectly.

"Marie," he said, "I'm going to pray for you." He opened his arms like Santa Claus at Christmas and said, "I want to hug you." He squeezed a good bit of himself through the open window and hugged me. My COVID mask was down around my neck, and my hand sanitizer was beside me in the console. There was complete silence around us. In my rearview mirror, I saw the horrified face of the man in the car behind me, but he did not beep.

As Jason released me and stood up, I said, "I'll pray for you too," and drove away.

God bless Jason, and God bless Joe, in Jesus's holy name. Amen.

25 Joe Is Still with Me

It has been a long time and a short time since Joe's death. The perception depends on the day, the atmospheric pressure, the method used to tell time, or many other variables. Looking back, time is fleeting. Looking forward without him, time drags its feet into eternity. I remember being with Joe's friends and our family after his memorial service at the Vienna Inn. Several of his friends had reported feeling his presence at odd times. One of them asked if I had experienced that yet. I had not.

"You will," he said, "and when you do, you'll know it's him."

God has been good to give me several of those moments in the last few years.

We were coming back from a funeral in June of 2019. Jim and I were silent on the two-hour trip home. I was playing Scrabble on my phone when I suddenly thought of that conversation I'd had with my son when I said, "You don't even like us, Joe."

My heart lurched, and as I looked out my window at the dark and dreary day, a muddy black pickup truck came alongside us on the right. As it pulled ahead, staying in the right lane, I noticed that someone had written "I LOVE YOU, MOM" on the dust-caked back window with a finger.

I caught my breath. It was a Joe moment, the pure connection of a message to me that I will treasure forever.

We were in Florida in January of 2020, and I talked Jim into going for a drive without a specific destination in mind. We talked about getting lunch and eating it at a beach, any beach.

Without intent, we wandered around in the car until we happened to see the Ritz Carlton. Jim decided to leave the car with the valet and find the beach-food shack. We walked through the lobby to Vanderbilt Beach and discovered that the beach shack in the dunes was jam-packed. There was a forty-minute wait for a seat, but a nice breeze and a sunny sky invited us to hang around.

As we shuffled out of the crowd of people in line to eat at a high table with a view, one of the waitstaff called us back. "There's a low table available over here if you want it." We did want it; in fact, we were stunned that there was a place for us.

Jim looked at me and said, "Isn't it strange that there was no place to sit, and this table suddenly became available? Clearly, there are people all around us who are still waiting."

I sat down and thought about our good fortune. Who would care that we'd found a special place to eat lunch on our vacation, I wondered.

"Joe would." The words reverberated in my heart. The thought surprised me, but it was so strong I decided to believe it. Why not? We love our son, and we believe he knew he was loved, and he would have reconciled with us if he'd lived.

The first day of June in 2021, I woke up happy—I'd been in the middle of a conversation with Joe, my first since his death. I didn't really see him, but I experienced his presence as a flash of recognition when I awoke, and he was in my peripheral vision, tan, young, and healthy, wearing a ski sweater I didn't recognize. It was striped, and one of the colors was a blue-green as luminescent as a tropical sea. He was wearing a matching hat too. I wish I knew what we were talking about because we were laughing.

I got up and took our dog, Sophie, for a walk. We ambled along, enjoying the breeze and the mist of recent rain. A memory of Joe, young, in high school, came to mind. We were on a plane, going to Hawaii for vacation. He was watching a *60 Minutes* segment being shown on the back of the seat in front of him. The plane wasn't even half full, so we were allowed to move around. I had gone back and slipped into a seat next to Joe for a while. He motioned for me to watch the show. It was about high school kids taking anabolic steroids, and it showed a gym where young men were injecting each other.

"Remember when you got mad at me because I quit working out at the gym," Joe said. "They were shooting each other in the butt, Mom. That's what was happening there, and you got mad at me when I stopped going."

I don't remember the rest of that conversation, but I know I was pleased that he was not doing steroids and sorry I had not trusted him enough to know that he was capable of making good decisions for himself.

A few days later, I was alone in the house, getting ready for a dental appointment. I decided to grab a quick bowl of cereal before I left. It felt right to say grace out loud. I surprised myself with words from the Lord's Prayer. When I got to "forgive us our trespasses," I said, "Please forgive me, God, for not letting Joe come home when I knew he was sick and without hope. Please, God, forgive me for closing the door on him because of my anger. I will repent and regret those cold words every day for the rest of my life. Thank you, God, for giving up your life on the cross for my sins. Help me to forgive others completely, the way you forgive me. The last thing I ever wanted to do was hurt you by hurting your precious creation, our son, Joe. Thank you, Lord, for saving him and loving him. Please make him aware of how much I love him."

I got in the car and went a little too fast because I was going to be late for the appointment. I was going to a periodontist, not my regular dentist, and I had never been to this location. I pulled off the busy road onto a side street. As soon as I programmed my phone's GPS, it announced "Arrived." I looked up and realized that the sign and the address on the building were the same as the information in my phone.

What a gift from my son, I thought. *An unexpected kindness to make my day easier. God bless him.*

I am becoming more aware of good things when they happen, and I credit Joe with putting them in my life. I also look for opportunities to do good deeds in Joe's honor so that other people are the beneficiaries of random acts of kindness. All of it helps me feel good.

At the end of my appointment, the doctor said, "I'll see you in six months."

The nurse opened her appointment book and said, "That will be in December. How do you feel about the sixteenth?"

"The sixteenth of December is my son's birthday," I said. "I like that day. I'll see you then."

"That is so sweet," she said.

I made it to the car before I cried, but they were happy tears. Joe and I are on the same page these days.

I remember that dream I had, the night before that fateful phone call that changed our lives. I remember surrendering my son to God, and I remember that little voice asking, "Even unto death?" I remember the pain that sent me to Urgent Care. I think I experienced some of the turmoil Joe was going through that night, and I trust in the Lord with all my heart, leaning not on my own understanding.

In a way, I feel I am like Abraham. He was willing to give up his son to God, and Isaac stayed with him. I gave up my son, Joe, and although this story had a different ending, in a sense he, too, is still with me.

THE END

Acknowledgments

The encouragement of my original editor, Jorge Hernandez, made this book a possibility. I am grateful for his support. Kristi Overton Johnson's decision to put my story in *Victorious Living* magazine gave me the courage to sift through the boxes of memories swirling through the storeroom in my mind until I found the real story. Thank you, Kristi, for helping me move forward and for introducing me to Wordscapes editor, Rachel Overton (no relation). Rachel was good cop and bad cop, patient and professional, whatever was necessary to keep the train moving. It could not have happened without her, because I was not ready to "let it go."

Peace did not come into my heart until I realized I did not have the power to create a perfect book, and I stopped trying. I gave the book to Jesus, and things fell into place immediately.

Terri Friedman, a friend from Wilkes University days (who is a former teacher, now full-time writer) introduced me to Demi Stevens, (also known as the Book Whisperer). During the pandemic, Demi created a library class to help people publish books. She has now helped more than 500 people publish. I sent her my book… and she read it immediately. There I was, blessed again. Thank you, Demi, for bringing *Forever in Our Hearts* to life.

Thank you to my mentor at Wilkes, Dr. J. Michael Lennon, for pushing me to write. And thank you to the professors and students at Wilkes for the atmosphere of collaboration that celebrates every student's achievement. I am so proud of my time with you.

Thank you to my daughters, Tammy Hooker Wolbert and Jennifer Lucile Hooker, for being the best friends, supporters, and encouragers that exist in the whole world. And thank you to my husband Jim, who has been unfailingly optimistic about whatever I do. God bless my family. It is perfect for me.

About the Author

MAUREEN O'NEILL HOOKER grew up in Newport, Rhode Island. In 1965, she married her Naval officer husband, Jim. Maureen worked in real estate for thirty years. When she was diagnosed with breast cancer and subsequent heart failure, she took a long look at her bucket list and finished her degree in psychology and literature at George Mason University. From there, she went on to Wilkes University, where she earned an MFA in Creative Writing.

In 2011, at the age of sixty-nine with no expectation of receiving a donor heart or ever being well again, Maureen received a call from the transplant team at Washington Medstar Heart and Vascular Institute. In 2017, she published her first book, *Shelly's Heart*, which chronicles her heart transplant experience. All proceeds from that book go directly to the Shelly Whitman Scholarship, created to help children of organ donors at East Carolina University.

On December 29, 2018, her son Joe, after a battle with multiple myeloma, took his own life. This raw and honest book tells her story of coming to terms with Joe's choice and his death.